Valeur et Discipline 1

Napoleonic Wars

Chasseurs à cheval of *Napoleon's Guard*

ANDREA PRESS

Publishing manager:
Javier Huerta

Text:
Miguel Ángel Martín Más

Illustrator:
Dionisio Álvarez Cueto
www.dionisioalvarez.com

Design and layout:
Voj Media Design S.L.
www.vojmedia.com

Translation:
Michael Oliver

Printing:
Printing Media

Edited by Andrea Press:
ANDREA PRESS
C/ Talleres, 21 - Pol. Ind de Alpedrete
28430 Alpedrete (Madrid)
Tel.: 918 57 00 08 - Fax: 918 57 00 48
www.andrea-miniatures.com
andrea@andrea-miniatures.com

ISBN: 84-96527-97-2

Contents

"THE BEST REGIMENT IN THE WORLD"

FORMATION AND ORGANIZATION

▲ Napoleon Bonaparte on the battlefield of Eylau, 1807. Bottom right can be seen two Chasseurs of the Guard acting as escorts to the Emperor. Oil on canvas by Antoine Jean Gros.

Following the Battle of Eylau on 7th - 8th February 1807, Napoleon visited his army on the battlefield to thank them for the terrible sacrifices they had made. As he walked between the ranks, shaking hands and slapping shoulders, calling his soldiers "My invincibles" and expressing his grief for all those who had fallen in the bloody combat, Napoleon heard how General Lasalle, who had been recognised with the command of an entire cavalry division, complained about not having being given command of the regiment of *Chasseurs à cheval de la Garde Impériale*.

"What's this?" the Emperor asked him "you do not seem satisfied."
"I feel flattered by your generosity, Sire," answered Lasalle," but I am not satisfied. I hoped that Your Majesty would choose me to command the best regiment in the world. Briefly, I thought that I was going to replace General Dahlmann in command of the *Chasseurs à cheval* of the Imperial Guard."
"When General Lasalle stops drinking, swearing and smoking," the Emperor responded, "not only will I put him in command of the *Chasseurs à cheval* of my Guard, but I will turn him into one of my chamberlains."

Antoine-Charles-Louis Lasalle. In spite of being one of the most gifted and audacious cavalry commanders, his undisciplined character precluded him from commanding Napoleon's Guard *Chasseurs à Cheval*.

Guidon of Bonaparte's *Guides* with the victories of the first Italian campaign embroidered on it. (Anne S. K. Brown Collection, Providence, USA).

Lasalle courteously inclined his head, replying:

> "Sire, since, according to you, I have all the attributes of a sailor, perhaps I should request the command of a frigate."
> "Oh, no!" responded the Emperor with an outburst of laughter, "that is not my wish. You will command twenty cavalry regiments in the absence of Prince Murat, who has returned to his duchy."

It was indisputably the undisciplined, impetuous character of Lasalle, otherwise probably the most talented light cavalry leader of the Napoleonic Wars, that caused Napoleon to consider him inappropriate for command of the 'elite of elites', the *Chasseurs à cheval de la Garde Impériale*, the Emperor's habitual escort and a valuable cavalry reserve in battle. It was a unit formed of

Napoleon at Malmaison. The Emperor's preferred uniform was the dress coat of a colonel of *Chasseurs* of the Guard, like the one shown here. This was also the uniform he wished to be buried in. (Oil on canvas by Jean Baptiste Isabey).

light cavalrymen of proven courage but also of outstanding moral fibre who had to serve as an example to the rest of the army. The following pages recount the history of this legendary unit –a unit whose antecedents are traced back to the first battles won by Napoleon in Italy and to the burning sands of the Egyptian desert. Indeed, a unit that paid the price demanded by glory and the ignominy of war, with its blood spilled on the plateaus of Austerlitz, the frozen countryside of Prussia and on the streets of Madrid, and many other places etched in the memory of those far off times.

Each member, like Napoleon, was an old hero who had confronted and conquered the fear of death. Their memory continues to inspire the modern would-be hero, who must accept a life where the opportunity no longer exists to partake in such a glorious adventure.

FORMATION AND ORGANIZATION

On 2nd of March 1796, the Directory of the French Republic appointed a young general, Napoleon Bonaparte, Commander-in-Chief of the Army of Italy. This young artillery officer had quickly advanced following his actions at the Siege of Toulon and again following the events in Paris on 13 Vendemaire 1795 - during which he repressed, with the infamous "whiff of grapeshot", a revolt that threatened the safety of the members of the Directory. He was placed in control of about 40,000 men, with whom he was to cross the Alps and enter Piedmont. The objective was to expel the Austrians from the fertile, rich territories of Italy, and send back substantial contributions and resources, like booty, to the impoverished, post-revolutionary France. After just three months of continuous operations and fighting, Bonaparte entered Milan victorious, having overcome the Austrians at Montenotte, Millesimo, Dego, Mondovi and Lodi. On 30th of May 1796, following the Battle of Borguetto, the triumphant French army was sent in pursuit of the Austrian infantry, which was, by then, in full retreat. The French Commander-in-Chief, consumed by fever and exhaustion after innumerable days with little sleep, crossed the river Mincio and lodged in a large house located on the bank of that river, near the outskirts of the small village of Valeggio. Once he had issued pertinent orders to his staff officers, Bonaparte could take off his boots and finally introduce his sore feet to an earthenware bowl of hot water. The general's rest would not, however, last long as, while his feet were soaking, a detachment of Austrian light cavalry that had become lost during the general dispersion of its army, advanced above the river looking for a ford to enable them return to the main body of their forces. An alert sentry guarding the door of the French Commander-in-Chief's lodgings, saw them arrive and promptly reacted, raised the alarm and closed the door behind him. Bonaparte went to the window and,

▲ Chasseur of the Imperial Guard. This is a contemporary illustration showing a Chasseur in the uniform '*à la chasseur*'. It consists of a green dress coat with long aprons or *habit*, with an aiguillette on the left shoulder, scarlet vest and green trousers adorned with Hungarian knots in *aurore*. The *colback* is the model used during the Empire period, with *raquettes,* tricolour cockade and red over green plume on the left side. He carries a carbine equipped with a bayonet, first issued in September 1803, and the model of sabre specially designed for this elite unit. (Henschell Collection, Kunstbibliothek, Berlin).

Formation of four squadrons of Chasseurs of the Imperial Guard. This unit was created in 1804, being the descendant of Bonaparte's *Guides* and the *Chasseurs* of the Consular Guard. (Illustration by Dionisio Álvarez Cueto). ▼

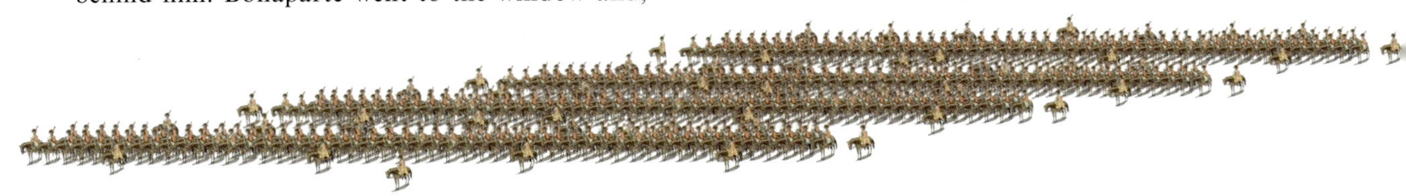

▲ Bessières, Marshal of the Empire and Commander-in-Chief of the cavalry of the Imperial Guard. (Engraving by L. Lacoste and L. Demoraine, The McGill University Napoleonic Collection).

imagining himself a captive of the Austrians, was determined that the campaign, crowned with so many victories, would not finish in so ridiculous a manner. Counting on a handful of soldiers who happened to be nearby, the general chose the "every man for himself" scenario, and departed hurriedly by the back door, leaving behind his boots and running barefoot with all speed into the garden where he mounted his horse and escaped by the skin of his teeth. On reaching Valeggio, where a contingent of French troops was quartered, he sent them immediately against the Uhlans who had been on the verge of capturing him.

This incident precipitated in Bonaparte a deep disquiet. He quickly came to the conclusion that he must be determined to prevent a reoccurrence of such an event in the future. In consequence, he decided on the creation of a special dedicated unit to attend to the monitoring and protection of the army's headquarters during the course of the campaign in addition to his own personal security. The unit would consist of both infantry and cavalry units. The former would be composed of members of the 6th and 7th battalions of Grenadiers under the command of the brigade commander, Jean Lannes; while the latter would comprise fifty sabres of light cavalry, selected for their bravery and discipline and commanded by Captain Jean Baptiste Bessières, of the *22e Chasseurs à cheval*, who would organize them. So was born the company of *Guides à cheval du Général en Chef de l'armée d'Italie*. From that moment, the new unit would dedicate itself to the protection of General Napoleon Bonaparte. In fact, there already existed a unit in the Army of Italy with this mission. A decree of the Legislative Assembly of 27th April 1792, had established the creation of a company of *Guides* à *Pied* and another of mounted *Guides à cheval* to be used for protecting the headquarters and the army's baggage. However, both units were engaged in activities inconsistent with the intent of the decree: the *Guides* à *Pied* were in Milan, guarding the archives and General Staff supplies, or being monopolized by the staff officers as *aides*. However, from June 1796, Bonaparte would never again be without his personal protective screen. In the coming years, from the desert sands to the roads of Europe, he would be surrounded by a select group of guards whose allegiance was to him alone and who would lay down their lives without hesitation in preserving that of their commander.

In his own inimitable style, Bonaparte immediately set things in motion. On 1st June 1796, he wrote to Captain Bessières, the recently appointed squadron commander of the *Guides à cheval*: "*The company of Guides à cheval, presently at the headquarters in Peschiera, must march tomorrow with all its arms and baggage, to Milan, where it will be equipped by him [Bessières] with uniforms, arms and all the equipment that it needs. The commander in command of this company will not withhold any effort to obtain the necessary items in the shortest possible time and will be considered responsible if by some negligence this unit is not equipped to the required standard.* While a great responsibility thus fell on Bessières, Bonaparte was sure that he was amply suited to the task, as his commander of the *Guides à cheval* had been carefully chosen. Bessières had demonstrated his boldness and value when he had led a charge against an Austrian artillery battery and had been fervently recommended by his friend and countryman, Joachim Murat, Bonaparte's favourite *aide de camp*.

It appears that, from the first moment, the *Guides à cheval* became the "beloved children" of Napoleon. They would receive the best provisions and would be the unit to which the army's finest cavalrymen would be sent, including the best of Bessières' old regiment, *22e Chasseurs à cheval*. However, it was not Bonaparte's intention to have merely a praetorian guard. The *Guides à cheval* also would be used as a strategic reserve for critical moments of a battle and would be able to restore a situation before the outcome of the battle was jeopardized.

At the end of September 1796, the company of *Guides à cheval* increased its complement to 160 men. In the succeeding months, the incorporation of new elements forced the creation of four squadrons, each one of which was granted a *guidon*, pennants on which their exploits would be embroidered.

Napoleon's first campaign in Italy –which would last until October 1797– presented the *Guides à cheval* with an opportunity to demonstrate that they were not merely useful for escort work, but that they also constituted a valuable battle unit; in fact, the intervention of a group of these valiant men in the battle of Arcole was a decisive factor in the subsequent victory. The company of *Guides à cheval du Général en Chef de l'armée d'Italie* presaged the future creation of the almost mythical regiment of the *Chasseurs à cheval de la Garde Impériale.* This guard regiment, that would attain such high levels of glory in the campaigns of the Empire, was essentially formed from the nucleus of the *Guides* and the foundation of its future formation was laid down in Italy.

Guides à cheval of the Army of the East

On 18th May 1798, Napoleon decided to resign from the mission assigned by the Directory –the invasion of the British Isles– and set course for Egypt to undertake another, less dangerous campaign but one that was also likely to deliver a telling blow to British pride and prestige. For the ensuing

Guide of the Commander-in-Chief of the Army of Italy, 1796. He wears the uniform *'à la chasseur'* adopted by Bonaparte's *Guides* at their creation. On his head he wears a low bicorne hat with an unpronounced arch that is markedly different from that used later during the Empire period, which had a much higher arch. The decoration on the uniform, such as the aiguillette, chevrons and piping were in *aurore*, that would continue to be used being on the uniforms of the *Chasseurs à Cheval* of both the Consular and Imperial Guard. The braids were worn by all the light cavalry of the republican period. He was armed with one of the many variants of light cavalry sabre Model 1776. (Illustration by D. A. C.).

Trompette of the Corps of *Guides* of the Eastern Army, 1798. The *Trompettes* of the Corps of Guides began by wearing the same green uniforms as rest of the troopers. However, in 1799, this was changed to the flamboyant sky blue uniform with crimson and sky blue plume that, according to to Trompette Krettly in its memoirs, drew the attention of and English admiral who asked to talk with the French during the Egyptian campaign. The *Trompette* is armed with the Model 1776 light cavalry sabre. (Illustration by D. A. C.).

Egyptian and Syrian campaigns, Napoleon took with him a cadre of *Guides à cheval.* This was formed from veterans of Italy and some new recruits - this Corps would receive the title of *Guides à cheval de l'Armée d'Orient*. It comprised ten companies: four of horse, one auxiliary mounted company, three of foot and two auxiliary foot companies. In addition there would be sixty artillerymen, a General Staff and twenty musicians.

The Egyptian campaign ended in fiasco. While, it is true that Bonaparte won several battles against the Mamelukes and Turks, on 1st August 1798 a British naval squadron destroyed the fleet of ships he had used to transport his army to those exotic lands. A year later, Bonaparte returned to France. Because of the shortage of ships, only 180 cavalry and 125 infantry from the *Guides* could return with him; all were selected from the longest serving and those most devoted to the general. The remainder were left behind to seek their fate in Egypt. On 16th October, Bonaparte arrived in Paris, where his astuteness at propaganda turned his great military failure in Egypt into a failure of the government. This allowed him to orchestrate a *coup d'etat* against the Directory on 10th November 1799, resulting in Napoleon becoming First Consul on 15th December. Those members of the *Guides à cheval* that had managed to return from the sands of the Egyptian desert were summoned to Paris, where they would resume the protection of their General, now the country's de facto Head of State.

Chasseurs à cheval of the Consular Guard

A decree of 28th November 1799 established the organization of the Consular Guard although, at that time, it was not considered necessary to create a company of *Chasseurs à cheval*. A later decree, of 3rd January 1800, established a company of this type from the two squadrons of Horse Grenadiers who had been the Directory Guard. Comprising four officers and 113 *Chasseurs*, under the command of Napoleon's stepson, Captain Eugène de Beauharnais, this company also accepted many veteran *Guides à cheval* from the Italian and Egyptian campaigns. So it was that the *Chasseurs à cheval de la Garde des Consuls*

Chasseur of the Consular Guard in a uniform *'à la hussarde'* in 1803. The uniform *'à la hussarde'* with its distinctive feature of the fur-edged pelisse began to be worn by the *Chasseurs* of the Guard from the end of 1800. (Engraving by E. Detaille, Vinkhuijzen Collection of Military Uniforms, New York Public Library).

Squadron Commander Beauharnais. The *schabraque* covering the saddle ridge is of green cloth with gold embroidery in an Eastern style, something that would only be allowed for this particular officer, as the other officers had one of the same cloth but without the exotic embroidery. At that time, the troopers had sheepskin *schabraques*. Once the pelisses were introduced the gauntlets were discarded as the fur trim prevented them from being pulled up and, therefore, the use of gloves became widespread among the *Chasseurs*. (Illustration by Benigni, taken from a contemporary engraving by Isabey. The Author's collection).

was born. The overall command of the cavalry of the Consular Guard –two squadrons of Horse Grenadiers and the company of *Chasseurs*– would fall to *Chef-de-brigade* Bessières, who had been the organizer of the first company of *Guides à cheval* in Italy in 1796.

In the middle of May 1800, the company of *Chasseurs à cheval de la Garde des Consuls* crossed the San Bernardo alpine pass in Bonaparte's company. On the 14th June, the company charged at Marengo, where almost half its complement was lost, killed or wounded.

On its return to Paris, a consular decree of 8th September 1800 transformed the company into a squadron of two companies totalling 234 men. On 9th May 1801, the *Chasseurs* received one hundred horses for guard services with thirty-six grooms to see to their care.

A decree of the 6th August 1801 formalized the creation of two squadrons of *Chasseurs à cheval de la Garde des Consuls* each comprising two companies.

▲
Colonel Eugène Beauharnais at the head of the *Chasseurs à Cheval* of the Consular Guard. This is a contemporary engraving that offers a clear overview of the new uniform *'à la hussarde'* adopted by the Consular Guard in 1800. At that time, it would have been used for parades and as the full dress uniform. In addition, accompanying this uniform is a *sabretache* with republican motifs while it is also a primary source confirming the use of red trousers at that time for full dress uniform. The white fur on the pelisses of the people in direct attendance to Beauharnais indicates that they are all officers. Beauharnais and one of the officers wear the white plume on the *colback* indicating that they belong to the Regimental General Staff. (Coloured engraving by N. Hoffmann, Anne S. K. Brown Collection).

The Each squadron staff consisted of a *Chef d'escadron*, an *Adjutant-major*, two *Porte-étendards*, a *Brigadier-trompette* and four *Maîtres-ouvriers*. At the end of September 1801, a second contingent of *Guides à cheval* managed to return to France from Egypt and their members were immediately transferred to both squadrons of *Chasseurs.*

A further decree, of 14th November 1801, granted the *Chasseurs à cheval* the title of "regiment" under the command of a brigadier although, provisionally, it would consist by just two squadrons commanded by the squadron commander, Beauharnais. On 8th March 1802, another directive reorganized the Consular Guard; the regiment of *Chasseurs à cheval* would continue to consist of two squadrons but with a considerably increased Staff: in addition, another four standard bearers were added along with a trumpet major (*Trompette-major*), two trumpeters and a drummer (*Timbalier*). The First Consul reserved the right to appoint the brigadier and staff officers when the regiment reached its full complement and, on 1st October 1802, it was ordered that the regiment should consist of four squadrons. With that, the total strength became fifty-six officers and 959 *Chasseurs*. On 13th October, Beauharnais was promoted to Brigadier with the command of four squadron commanders: Morland, Dahlmann, Beurmann and Hercule – this last a black lieutenant who was the hero of Arcole. Morland was promoted Major (corresponding to the rank of lieutenant-colonel in a line regiment) on 21st January 1804. This same decree assigned a company of Mamelukes to the *Chasseurs à cheval de la Garde des Consuls*.

Chasseurs à cheval of the Imperial Guard

On the 18th May 1804, the Senate proclaimed Napoleon Emperor of France, although the coronation ceremony would not take place until 2nd December. Simultaneously, the Consular Guard received the title of Imperial Guard. A decree of 29th July 1804 confirmed the new title and fixed the composition of the regiment at four squadrons plus the company of Mamelukes.

The nominal command of the regiment, as *Colonel-géneral* of *chasseurs*, would remain with Eugène de Beauharnais, although he was promoted to brigadier-general on 6th March 1805, major-general a few days later and Viceroy of Italy on 13th May of that same year. On this date, effective command of the regiment devolved to General Morland, who was also awarded the rank of *Colonel-Commandant*, whilst Dahlman was promoted to *Major*. After the death of Morland at Austerlitz, Dahlmann became *Colonel-Commandant* with Guyot as *Major*.

A directive of 17th September 1805 created four companies of *vélites* (cadets) for the *Chasseurs à cheval*, grouped into a single squadron. On 15th April 1806, a further directive ordered the reorganization of the Guard. This required the formation of two squadrons of *vélites* numbered 5 and 6 of the regiment under the command of a single squadron commander. The function of the *vélites* was to replace any losses in the first four squadrons in order to maintain a constant complement of 250 men in each. At this time, the regiment consisted of seventy officers and 1,239 *Chasseurs*.

In 1806, Dahlmann left the *Chasseurs* and command of the regiment devolved to the *Major* (Guyot). On 16th February 1807, Squadron Commander Thiry was named second *Major*. On 18th January 1808, Brigadier-General Lefèbvre-Desnoëttes was appointed *Colonel-Commandant*. This was after a year without the regiment actually coming under his command. It is probable that, on that date, Beauharnais stepped down as *Colonel-géneral* of the regiment, although it is not known for sure. When Lefèbvre Desnoëttes was taken prisoner in Spain by the British on 29th December 1808, "*Colonel-Géneral*" became a mere nominal position since, of course, he could not command from his captivity in England.

On 11th January 1809, the *Chevaux-légers* of the Grand Duke of Berg (Murat's old *Guides à cheval*) was assigned to the *Chasseurs à cheval* of the Guard. The same happened with Mortier's *Guides à cheval* on 1st February. On 5th June 1809, Major Guyot was promoted to *Colonel*

Chasseur of the Consular Guard in uniform '*à la chasseur*' 1803. This *chasseur* has protected his *colback* plume with a cover to avoid deterioration; he wears riding breeches with inner-leg leather reinforcements, a trooper's vest with only two rows of buttons – sergeant-majors and officers wore one with three or up to five rows of buttons– and he leans on his Model 1803 *Chasseurs-à-Cheval de la Garde* sabre. The saddle is equipped with the sheepskin *schabraque* used by troopers during the republican period. (Engraving by E. Detaille, Vinkhuijzen Collection of Military Uniforms, NYPL).

▲ The First Consul visits the Hospice of Mount San Bernardo. Beside Napoleon is the *colonel en second* of the Chasseurs à Cheval of the Guard. (Oil on canvas by Jacques Lebel, Musée National du Château, Versailles, France).

Lefèbvre-Desnöettes, in the uniform of Colonel of the *Chasseurs* of the Guard. (Watercolour attributed to William Heath, Anne S. K. Brown Collection). ▼

Commandant with Major Thiry being transferred to the Line as a Brigadier General. Meanwhile, the two squadron commanders, Daumesnil and Corbineau, were promoted *Majors* on 13th June. Following the Battle of Wagram, (9th August), Colonel Lion of the *14e Chasseurs à cheval* of the Line was promoted to the rank of third *Major* of the *Chasseurs à cheval* of the Guard.

On 1st August 1811, following the disbandment of the *vélites*, the regiment was reorganized into five squadrons. On the 16th December of that year, Brigadier General Guyot was promoted to Major General, although still retaining command of the *Chasseurs*. Also in 1811, Colonel d'Haugeranville and General Excelmans replaced Majors Corbineau and Daumesnil, both having had limbs amputated at the Battle of Wagram.

At the beginning of 1812, the regiment was formed of five squadrons plus the company of Mamelukes. On 6th May of that year, General Lefèbvre-Desnoëttes was reinstated as effective commander of the regiment after his escape from British captivity in England.

Chasseurs à cheval of the Old and Young Guard

After the disastrous campaign in Russia, the *Chasseurs* of the Guard saw their numbers decimated. This resulted in the decree of 18th January 1813 creating the Young Guard that added three more squadrons to the five existing before the 1812 fiasco. On 6th March, a further squadron was added - the 9th. Mamelukes would form the 10th squadron; the first time the company had been awarded the title of "Squadron".

Following the decree of 17th March 1813, the first five squadrons were slotted into the Old Guard and the other four into the Young Guard, with the following structure:

1st squadron: companies 1 and 6
2nd squadron: companies 2 and 7
3rd squadron: companies 3 and 8
4th squadron: companies 4 and 9
5th squadron: companies 5 and 10
6th squadron: companies 11 and 15
7th squadron: companies 12 and 16
8th squadron: companies 13 and 17
9th squadron: companies 14 and 18

The regiment remained united during the campaign of 1813, with Lefèbvre-Desnoëttes at its head, Major General Guyot as deputy commander and *Colonel-Majors* Lion and Meuziau in charge of the Old Guard and the Young Guard respectively.

In December 1813, the regiment divided: General Lion in command of the squadrons of the Old Guard, plus the 11th company of 6th squadron and the first company of Mamelukes departed to form part of the *Grande Armée* in Germany. Meanwhile, the 15th company of 6th squadron, 7th, 8th and 9th squadrons and the second company of Mamelukes remained in Belgium under the command of Lefèbvre-Desnoëttes.

Chasseurs of the Imperial Guard in *grande tenue de service* uniform, 1804-1815. The colback's white plume identifies one of the officers in as a member the Regimental General Staff. The officers' pelisses are trimmed with Arctic fox fur while those of the troops are trimmed with black sheepskin. The first figure shows an officer mounted on a sorrel horse with the other on a chestnut, the colours commonly used by this unit. (Watercolor by L. Rousselot, Anne S. K. Brown Collection).

At the end of December of that same year, the title of *2e Chasseurs à cheval* Regiment of the Imperial Guard or *Hussards Eclaireurs de la Jeune Garde* began to be applied to the 6th to 9th squadrons, although none of these titles ever became official.

The Royal Corps of Chasseurs à cheval of France

With the abdication of Napoleon on 6th April 1814 and the return of the Bourbons, the future of a regiment so closely allied to the name and person of the deposed Emperor did not appear to be very rosy. By the end of the 1814 campaign, the squadrons of the Old Guard totalled eighty-nine officers and 1,357 *Chasseurs.* However, a royal decree of 14th May 1814 would drastically reduce those numbers to forty-four officers and 641 *Chasseurs* and it would be reconstituted as the *Corps Royal des cheval Chasseurs de France*. The squadrons of the Young Guard were dissolved and their members transferred to the *Chasseurs à cheval* of the Line.

A further decree of the 26th June fixed the composition of the *Chasseurs à cheval* regiment of France to four squadrons of

Chasseur of the Young Guard in *tenue de campagne* uniform, 1813. The Young Guard recruits were young men offered to Napoleon by municipal corporations and departments of France. They were selected for their height, physical qualities and equestrian skills. The officers came from the Old Guard and must have completed twelve years service with four of these in the rank. (Watercolor by L. Rousselot, Anne S. K. Brown Collection).

two companies each. It also left Lefèbvre-Desnoëttes in overall command, with General Lion as Major of the regiment.

The One Hundred Days

After the Emperor escaped his exile on Elba and returned to France, the faithful veteran *Chasseurs à cheval* were delirious with joy and soon arranged to place themselves at the disposal of the Emperor. Around 400 veteran *Chasseurs* and a further ninety-four Mamelukes, who had been demobilized by the Bourbons, dusted off their old uniforms from their trunks and started on the road to the reconstruction of their beloved regiment.

A decree of 21st March 1815 restored the Imperial Guard and another, of 8th April established its composition. It was to remain as the *Chasseurs à cheval de la Garde* - a regiment consisting of four squadrons. A further decree of 15th May established the creation of a cavalry regiment of Young Guard to be assigned to the corps of *Chasseurs à cheval de la Garde* under the same command. It was formed in Paris under the orders of Lefèbvre-Desnoëttes, receiving the title *of 2e Regiment de Chasseurs à cheval de la Jeune Garde.* No Colonel of the regiment was designated and command fell to Merlin-de-Douai with the rank of Major.

The 1st regiment, that of the Old Guard, campaigned in Belgium and fought at Waterloo. However the 2nd regiment, the Young Guard, was without mounts from its inception and, at first, could not leave Chantilly. Following Napoleon's defeat on June 1815 by Wellington and Blücher, both regiments retired with the main body of the army towards the Loire. At the end of November, the 1st Regiment was disbanded in Périgueux. The 2nd was distributed across several other regiments and then disbanded days later.

Very few members of the *Chasseurs à cheval de la Garde* were permitted to serve in the French army after Napoleon's final defeat. No unit of the Imperial army had been so close to the Emperor throughout the various campaigns and their continued service became unthinkable unless it was in the service of the man who turned them into heroes. During the years of far-off exile on Saint Helena, Napoleon surely still remembered the names of many of the men to whom he trusted his life on so many occasions. While it impossible in the following pages put faces to all these names, we can tell of the commanders of the regiment and of some of the legendary personalities who could fill page upon page with their heroic deeds.

THE PERSONALITIES

Jean Baptiste Bessières (1768-1813)

The son of a surgeon, Bessières was on the brink of following his father into the medical profession when hard times and the Revolution took him away into armed service. His career began in the National Guard –of which he became captain of Grenadiers– that later was to form part of Louis XVI's Constitutional Guard. After the King's execution, he served in the Army of the Pyrenees, first as an infantryman, recovering his rank in 1793 and later serving as a captain in *22e Chasseurs à cheval*. Three years later, whilst still with the same regiment, he came under the command of General Bonaparte in Italy. The courage he demonstrated during a charge against an Austrian battery at Cremona and the friendship with his fellow Gascon, Joachim Murat, at that time an aide de camp to Bonaparte, were among the reasons for his promotion to commanding officer of the company of *Guides à cheval* of the Army of Italy. On 5th June 1796 he was named a provisional squadron commander and distinguished himself with the *Guides at* Rivoli and La Favorita. At the successful conclusion of the Italian campaign, Napoleon rewarded him by sending him to Paris with captured Austrian standards, a distinction whereby Bonaparte demonstrated his esteem for this valiant officer and the *Guides à cheval* that he commanded.

Promoted to *Chef de Brigade* on 9th March 1797, he served in the Egyptian campaign in command of the *Guides à cheval* of the Army of the East. On his return to France, as

▲ Napoleon at the Battle of Wagram, 6th July 1809. On the left is shown a *Chasseur* in a watchful pose and, on the right, the *Chasseur de portefeuille*; the trooper entrusted with carrying the leather bag containing the Emperor's military equipment and maps. The figure lying on the ground is Bessières, the Commander-in-Chief of the Cavalry of the Guard - he has been wounded, a fact that has caused great consternation among his men. (Oil on canvas by H. Vernet).

commander of the Guard of the Legislative Body, he supported Bonaparte in his *coup d'état* of 18 Brumaire. Soon after, he was awarded with the command of the Horse Grenadiers of the Consular Guard, which had just been created.

He returned to fight in Italy under Napoleon in 1800. Following the Battle of Marengo, he was promoted to *Général de Brigade* and sub-commander of the Consular Guard. By 1802 he was already a *Géneral de Division* and two years later he received the title of Marshal of the Empire, 14th in seniority, and command of the cavalry of the Imperial Guard.

He was to participate with distinction throughout the most important episodes of the wars of the Empire: the battles of Austerlitz, Jena, Eylau and Friedland, the War in Spain - where he won an important victory at Medina de Rio Seco on 24th July 1808 - the 1809 Austrian campaign and the disastrous 1812 Russian campaign.

Bessières, however, would not live to see the fall of the man who had turned him into a hero of France. On 1st May 1813 - the day before the battle of Lützen, while reconnoitring the defile of Poserna-Rippach, he was struck by a cannon ball and instantly killed.

▲
Jean Baptiste Bessières, Commander-in-Chief of the Cavalry of the Imperial Guard.

Eugène de Beauharnais (1781-1824)

The son of Josephine's first husband, General Alexandre de Beauharnais, who was guillotined in 1794, Eugène became Napoleon's stepson in May 1796. At the end of that same year, the young Beauharnais marched with General Masséna to Milan where he was named second lieutenant and aide de camp to the commander in chief. All of those with whom he served in the first Italian campaign, among them Joseph Bonaparte, the French ambassador to Rome, recognized his value, his generosity and the nobility of his character.

In 1798 he accompanied his stepfather on the Egyptian campaign, during which he was promoted to the rank of lieutenant and distinguished himself during the capture of the fortress of Acre. After returning to France and the *coup d'état* that made his stepfather First Consul, he was named captain in the *Chasseurs à cheval* of the Consular Guard. It was with this new rank that he set out to fight in the second Italian campaign. Thanks to the valour he demonstrated during the cavalry charge that led to the victory at Marengo, he was promoted to the rank of squadron commander. However, it was not only valour that he demonstrated, but also great humanity, when ordering the *Chasseurs* under his command to open their ranks during the charge and swerve to avoid a wounded Austrian, who had surrendered with raised hands. "You must respect the brave men that have fallen on misfortune", he said to his men. Beauharnais had become the epitome of a valiant and noble horseman, and an example to the rest of the elite troops that were the *Chasseurs à cheval de la Garde*. His stepfather had great plans for him.

▲
Eugène de Beauharnais, Commander-in-Chief of the *Chasseurs* of the Guard. This picture shows the mature Beauharnais, having already spent the glorious years of his youth as Commander-in-Chief of the *Chasseurs* of the Guard.

In 1802, he was promoted colonel and on 4th December 1803 received the title of *Chevalier* of the Order of the Legion of Honour. In 1804 he became a *Général-de-Brigade* and Commander-in-Chief of the *Chasseurs à cheval de la Garde*. On 14th June 1804 he was named Commander of the Order of the Legion of Honour, making him a Prince of France. Finally, on 1st February 1805, he received the title of Chancellor of State of the Empire. A sparkling career promoted by his mother's husband, the erstwhile General of the Republic, who had raised the Beauharnais family to be part of the Imperial family.

However, the titles and possessions that were added to the portfolio of the nominal commander of the *Chasseurs à cheval de la Garde Impériale* during those years did not end there. When France became an Empire in 1804, the Italian Republic –that had been created under the initiative and protection of Napoleon– ended up becoming a Vice-royalty that would be given to Beauharnais. It is probable that his appointment to Viceroy of Italy ended his relationship with the *Chasseurs à cheval de la Garde Impériale*.

Eugène de Beauharnais, Commander-in-Chief of the *Guides*, the Italian Campaign, 1799 –1800. (Vinkhuijzen Collection, NYPL).

Beauharnais returned to the battlefield for the Austrian campaign of 1809, distinguished himself at Borodino in 1812 and Lützen in 1814. He remained faithful to Napoleon until his first abdication in 1814, but he did not follow him after his return from Elba in 1815 as he had promised his father-in-law, the King of Bavaria, he would not return to involve himself in the affairs of France. He became Prince of Eichstadt and Duke of Leuchtenberg, and lived the remainder of his life in Munich, dedicated to helping his stepfather's veterans and servicemen who had been abandoned after the second abdication.

MORLAND'S CORPSE

Little is known concerning Morland, the first *Major* of the *Chasseurs à cheval* of the Imperial Guard, but paradoxically, the destiny of his corpse is well recorded, thanks to the Memoirs of Baron de Marbot:
"Of all the units of the Imperial Guard, the *Chasseurs à Cheval* suffered more losses in the great charge against the Russian Guard on the Pratzen Heights. My poor friend, Fournier, was killed, as was General Morland. It is said that Napoleon intended to inter General Morland in a mausoleum that was to be constructed in the middle of the esplanade of *Les Invalides*. With this in mind the corpse was conserved in a barrel of rum. However, the mausoleum was never built, and it is said that the body of the General was still in a room of the Medical School when Napoleon lost his Empire in 1814."

Nicolas Dahlmann (1769-1807)

Dahlmann, son of a trumpeter of the *Dauphin Cavalerie* regiment, was readied for service in that same unit as an *enfant de troupe* in 1777 at the age of eight. After the Revolution, he served in the Army of the Moselle and that of the Eastern Pyrenees. In 1796, he marched to Italy with Bonaparte's troops and there he was one of those selected to make up the company of *Guides* of the Army of Italy, ending the campaign with the rank of second lieutenant. He joined the *Guides* of the l'Armee d'Orient, distinguishing himself in Salahieh –where he won a battlefield promotion to lieutenant– and Aboukir. One of the lucky ones to return to France with the commander-in-chief after the *l'Armee d'Orient* was abandoned in Egypt, Dahlmann was named squadron commander of the *Chasseurs à cheval* of the Consular Guard in October 1802. He served at Austerlitz, where, at the head of two squadrons of *Chasseurs*, he captured 1,500 prisoners and twenty guns. He gained the rank of colonel of *Chasseurs à cheval de la Garde Impériale* when the previous colonel, François-Louis Morland, was killed in that battle.

On 30th November 1806, after notably participating in the Battle of Jena and the Battle of Lopaczyn, the Emperor promoted him to *Général-de-brigade*, an appointment that forced him to leave the *Chasseurs à cheval de la Garde Impériale*.

Nicolas Dahlmann, Squadron Commander, 1802-1805 and Colonel of the regiment, 1805-1806.

▲
Nicolas Dahlmann as Colonel of the *Chasseurs* of the Imperial Guard, 1806. (Illustration by E. L. Bucquoy. The Author's collection).

At the Battle of Eylau, 8th February 1807, he requested the honour of being united with his old regiment for a charge. He died, as he would have wanted, next to his old comrades in arms, a large-calibre cannon ball destroying his left hip.

Frédéric Auguste Beurmann (1777-1815)

Beurmann began his military career as a simple soldier a few years before the French Revolution. In 1792, he was already a second lieutenant and, the following year, an *aide-de-camp* to General Kléber. In 1795, he joined the *Chasseurs à cheval* as a first lieutenant and, in 1798, became an aide-de-camp to General Mortier. In November 1800, he was transferred to the *Chasseurs à cheval* of the Consular Guard where he would become a squadron commander in 1802. He became prominent at the Battle of Austerlitz, refusing to leave the battlefield in spite of having received two bayonet thrusts that caused him to lose a considerable amount of blood. After convalescing, he left the *Chasseurs* to be promoted to colonel and took over command of the 17th Dragoons.

On 13th April 1815 he committed suicide with a shot to the head. With Napoleon's return to France, Beurmann could not face the shame of meeting Napoleon because of his supposed treason of accepting the title of *Chevalier* of the Meritorious Military Service Order from Louis XVIII.

Joseph Domingue "Hercule" (1761-1820)

The ideals of equality and the, hopefully proposed Declaration of the Rights of Man by the philosophers of the Revolution also arrived in the islands of the Caribbean, principally Haiti, where the numerous black slave population decided to fight for its much-desired freedom. It is, perhaps, this situation that precipitated the escape of a slave, Joseph Domingue, born in Havana in 1761, and his subsequent journey to Bordeaux. It is not known under what circumstances or what eventful journeys he took for such a distance. What is known with certainty is that, in the new Revolutionary France, skin color was no impediment to enlistment in the Infantry regiment of Champagne. In 1793 he joined the 22nd *Chasseurs à cheval* regiment that was integrated into the Army of the Eastern Pyrenees, formed to fight the Spanish in the War of the Convention. Domingue demonstrated audacity and valour in this campaign and he was promoted to *maréchal-des-logis* that, in the French cavalry of the time, was the equivalent of sergeant. He participated with his regiment in the first Italian campaign and was selected by Captain Bessières to join the *Guides*, in which he was promoted lieutenant on 26th October 1796. His uncommon strength –which earned him the nickname "Hercule"– and his bravery in the battle called him to the attention of Bonaparte who, after witnessing his heroic performance at Bassano, promoted him lieutenant and then, after the charge he led at Arcole, to captain. In addition, he was awarded a substantial financial allowance and a Sabre of Honour – the prize that had replaced medals, which the republicans had abolished considering them decorations of the Old Regime – with a motto recorded in the blade that said: "Pour avoir renversé, à tête de 25 guides, un colonne autrichienne à bataille d'Arcole" ("For forcing the retreat, at the head of 25 *Guides*, of an Austrian Column at the Battle of Arcole").

Hercules, despite his skin color and although practically illiterate, reached the field rank of squadron commander in the *Chasseurs à cheval* of the Consular Guard. He eventually left the regiment to take command of the *Pionniers Noirs*, a unit created from Haitian blacks who had been made prisoner by General Leclerc in 1802 after being sent to the island to quell the revolt of the slaves. It appears that Hercules was not greatly pleased by the change. This is perfectly understandable, as he had belonged to one of the most prestigious units in the army –and, without a doubt, closest to Napoleon– to command a group of ex-slaves forced to become soldiers and in charge of heavy work, such as digging or deactivating grenades and shells. Napoleon, in order to placate him, agreed to grant an Eagle to his Pioneer unit. However, he was so demoralised for a man accustomed to the glory of combat, that he obtained his discharge in 1805.

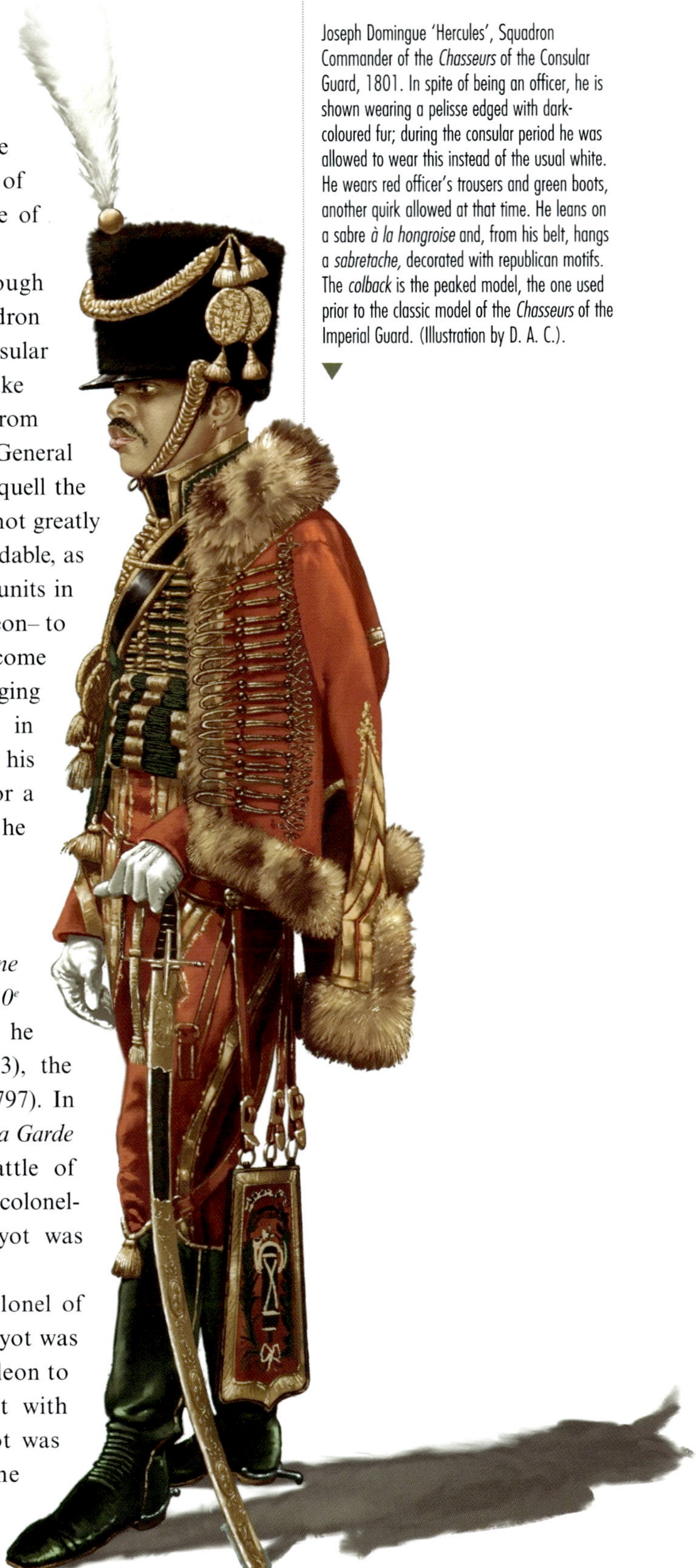

Joseph Domingue 'Hercules', Squadron Commander of the *Chasseurs* of the Consular Guard, 1801. In spite of being an officer, he is shown wearing a pelisse edged with dark-coloured fur; during the consular period he was allowed to wear this instead of the usual white. He wears red officer's trousers and green boots, another quirk allowed at that time. He leans on a sabre *à la hongroise* and, from his belt, hangs a *sabretache,* decorated with republican motifs. The *colback* is the peaked model, the one used prior to the classic model of the *Chasseurs* of the Imperial Guard. (Illustration by D. A. C.).

Claude Étienne Guyot (1769-1837)

Guyot enlisted in the *Chasseurs à cheval de Bretagne* on 1st November 1790. This later became the *10e Chasseurs à cheval* regiment. With this regiment he served in the campaigns on the Moselle (1793), the Vendée (1795), in Italy (1796) and Germany (1797). In October 1802 he joined the *Chasseurs à cheval de la Garde* with the rank of captain. Following the Battle of Austerlitz and the promotion of Dahlmann to colonel-major, owing to the death of Morland, Guyot was promoted major of the regiment.

In 1808, under the command of the new colonel of the regiment, General Lefèbvre Desnoëttes, Guyot was in charge of the escort that accompanied Napoleon to Spain. On 5th June 1809, after having fought with honour in the Battle of Aspern-Essling, Guyot was promoted to second-in-command of the *Chasseurs* and, on 9th August of that same year, to General-de-Brigade. This was

▲ Charles Lefèbvre-Desnoëttes. After being captured by the British at Benavente, they allowed his servants and baggage to accompany him into captivity. By so doing, he was able to wear the full dress uniform during supper that was given in his honour by General Moore. During the supper, Lefèbvre revealed his embarrassment of not being able to carry his sabre; the British general pulled one of his own from its scabbard and gave it to the Frenchman – an example of the high esteem in which one of the Napoleon's favourite generals was held.

followed a few days later by the award of the title Baron of the Empire. Finally, on 15th March 1810 he was named Chamberlain to the Emperor.

On 1st December 1813, Guyot left the *Chasseurs* to command the 1st regiment of Grenadiers of the Guard, which he would lead into battle at Waterloo and where he was twice wounded. After the fall of Napoleon he was retired from the service by the Bourbons. That, however, was not the end of his military career as, in 1830, he was appointed Commander of 16th Military District, with headquarters in Toulouse. He finally retired in 1833 and died in Paris four years later.

Charles Lefèbvre-Desnoëttes (1773-1822)

The young Charles, son of a draper in Paris and Army supplier, was, without doubt, much more interested in dressing up in a uniform than in selling the fabric necessary for its preparation. He left school three times to enlist. On the first two occasions, his well-off parents paid for his discharge but, on the third, they surrendered to the inevitable realising that their son's destiny lay in the army. The obstinate young soldier became, with time, an *aide-de-camp* to Napoleon when he was named First Consul. By 1806 he was already a *Général-de-brigade* rising to *Général-de-division* in 1807, and he was just thirty-four.

In January 1808 he was named Colonel of the *Chasseurs à cheval de la Garde Impériale*, leading them into Spain. He was taken prisoner by the British in the neighbourhood of Benavente on 29th December of that year. The British, conscious of the reputation of the famous general, did not accede to the normal interchange of prisoners and he was sent to England. He was destined to spend several years in the city of Cheltenham until, frustrated by inactivity, he broke his word of honour not to try to abscond and, in 1812, he escaped to return to France. Once there, he recovered command of the *Chasseurs à cheval de la Garde Impériale* and subsequently led them during the Russian campaign. He was wounded at Winkowo, but recovered in time to command the Emperor's escort during the famous retreat.

In 1813 he fought in Germany and took command of the cavalry of the Young Guard on 25th November of that year. He served in the 1814 France campaign during which he received two bayonet wounds at Brienne on 29th January 1814. He was still commanding the Emperor's escort after his abdication.

On receiving the news of Napoleon's return in 1815, Lefèbvre-Desnoëttes returned to the *Chasseurs à cheval*, which was stationed in Cambrai, and unsuccessfully attempted to take control of the arsenal at La Fère. He returned as Colonel of the *Chasseurs à cheval de la Garde Impériale* on 14th April 1815, and became a Peer of France on 2nd June. At Waterloo, he was to command the division of Light Cavalry of the Guard. After the return of the Bourbons, he was outlawed and forced to flee and live like a refugee in the United States. In 1822, returning to Europe, his boat was shipwrecked on the Irish coast and he drowned. At Kinsale, the place of the shipwreck, his widow had a lighthouse constructed to perpetuate his memory.

Pierre Daumesnil (1777-1832)

On 14th July 1794, a young, seventeen-year old boy, Pierre Daumesnil, fled his native Périgueux after having killed, in a duel, an artilleryman who had insulted him. He enlisted in *22e Chasseurs à cheval*, with whom he fought against the Spanish in the Rosellon during the two following years, being wounded in the combat of Delne on August 1794. At the beginning of 1796 he returned to his regiment, which was then sent to Italy. Captain Bessières, who was already well aware of his boldness and valour, being his superior officer in the *22e Chasseurs à cheval* when this regiment was integrated into the Army of the Eastern Pyrenees, selected him to form part, with the rank of *brigadier* (cavalry corporal), a select group of *Guides* of the Army of Italy. In 1798 he was promoted to *maréchal-des-logis* (cavalry sergeant). In the Egyptian campaign he came to the notice of General Bonaparte for his zeal in protecting him, covering him with his body on an occasion when an explosive grenade fell close by. Luckily, the projectile buried itself in the sand and did not explode, so Daumesnil survived to receive the nickname of "Guardian Angel of Bonaparte" and to distinguish himself once again during the attack on the fortress of San Juan de Acre, where he was wounded by a Turkish scimitar. For his heroic actions during the assault, Daumesnil received a Sabre of Honour.

Pierre Daumesnil, 'the Guardian Angel of Bonaparte'. (Engraving by Maurin. The Author's collection).

A man of such great value could not be left in the sands of the desert, so Daumesnil was one of those chosen to return to France with Bonaparte and to enlist in the *Chasseurs à cheval* of the Consular Guard in December 1799. Promoted to second lieutenant in April 1800, lieutenant in June and captain a year later, he reached his highest rank in the *Chasseurs à cheval de la Garde* on being promoted to squadron commander in 1805, after the Battle of Austerlitz. Later he participated in the campaigns in Prussia and Poland in 1806 and 1807 respectively.

In 1808 he was sent with the cavalry of the Imperial Guard to Spain and was almost killed in the streets of Madrid while leading his Mameluke and *Chasseur* squadron, during the rising of the 2nd May. In 1809 he was transferred to the Army of Germany and fought at Eckmühl and at Wagram. It was at the latter battle that his cavalry career came to an end when he lost a leg.

Napoleon was fully aware of the merit that Daumesnil had accumulated after so many years of active duty in his service, which he maintained in spite of the gravity of his wound.

In 1806, he was granted the title of Officer of the Legion of Honour followed, in 1810, by title of Baron of the Empire and, in 1812, the rank of *General-de-brigade* with the position of Governor of the Fortress of Vincennes.

In 1814, brave "*jambe-de-bois*" (wooden-leg), his new nickname, was still able to contribute to the epic of the Napoleonic Wars. On the night of the 30th/31st March, accompanied by his troops and 250 horses, he left Vincennes. It had been arranged to gather all the material and armament that had been distributed for the defence of Paris – that the signed capitulation of 30th March demanded should be given to the Allies - for storage in the fortress and then to refuse its delivery.

The Bourbon restoration named him Military Governor of the small town of Condé but, as soon as Napoleon recovered his throne in 1815, Daumesnil was returned to be governorship of the Fortress of Vincennes and, once again, would refuse to surrender it to the Prussian General Blücher after Napoleon's final defeat. Coincidentally, many years later in 1831, he defended the fortress against siege by an angry mob wanting the former Bourbon ministers in the government of Charles X.

Daumesnil died in his beloved Fortress of Vincennes, symbol of the resistance of Napoleon's supporters, on 17th August 1832. He who could not be brought down by sabre cuts, musket or cannon-fire, was finally taken by cholera.

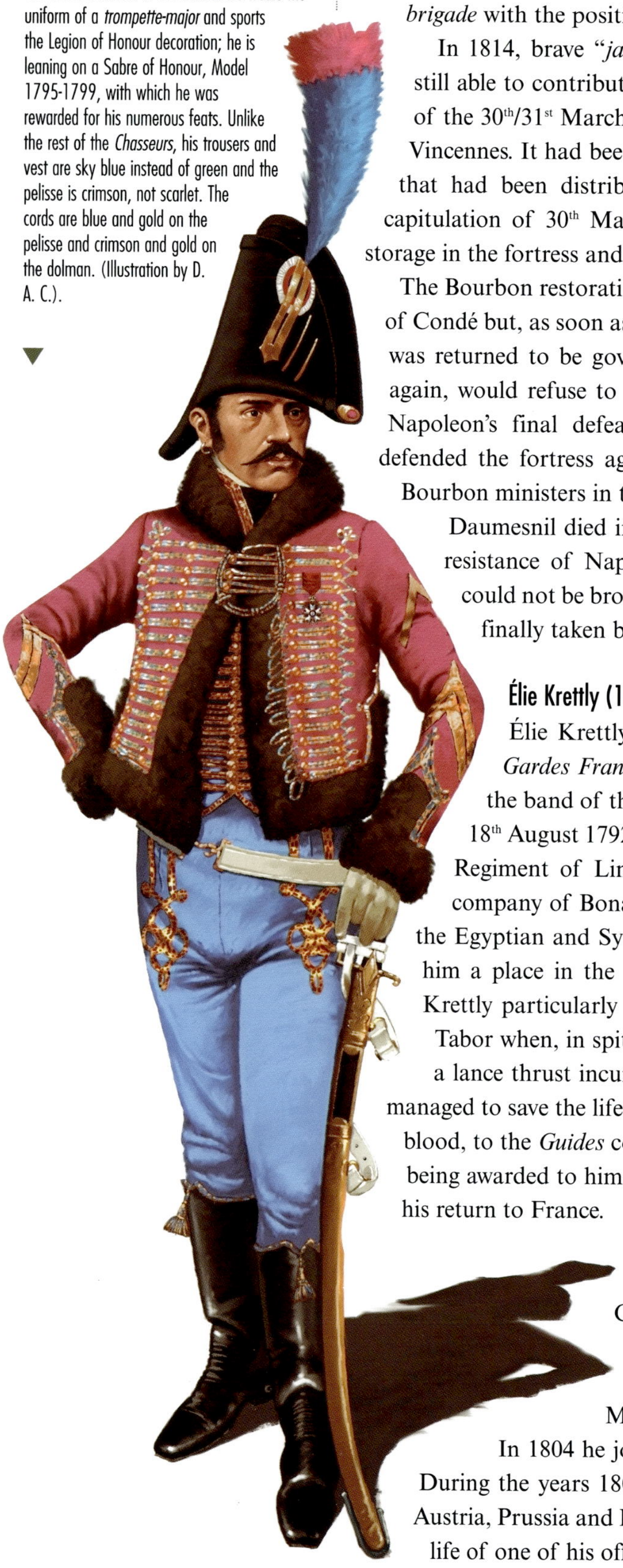

Élie Krettly, the most audacious *Trompette* of the *Chasseurs à cheval* of the Guard. He wears the uniform of a *trompette-major* and sports the Legion of Honour decoration; he is leaning on a Sabre of Honour, Model 1795-1799, with which he was rewarded for his numerous feats. Unlike the rest of the *Chasseurs*, his trousers and vest are sky blue instead of green and the pelisse is crimson, not scarlet. The cords are blue and gold on the pelisse and crimson and gold on the dolman. (Illustration by D. A. C.).

Élie Krettly (1775-1840)

Élie Krettly enlisted, on 5th January 1789, in the regiment of *Gardes Françaises.* On 31st August of that same year, he joined the band of the National Guard of Paris, in which he served until 18th August 1792, when he was transferred as a musician to the 104th Regiment of Line Infantry. He transferred as a trumpeter to the company of Bonaparte's *Guides* in September of 1797 and fought in the Egyptian and Syrian campaigns, during which his feats him gained him a place in the pantheon of the heroes of the Napoleonic Wars. Krettly particularly distinguished himself during the Battle of Mount Tabor when, in spite of being wounded by a bullet, a scimitar cut and a lance thrust incurred during the charges against the Mamelukes, he managed to save the life of Lieutenant Dahlmann and to return, covered in blood, to the *Guides* company. This action resulted in a Sabre of Honour being awarded to him and recognition by the First Consul Bonaparte on his return to France.

Named *brigadier-trompette* (chief-trumpeter) of the *Chasseurs à cheval* of the Consular Guard in December of 1799, he took part in the 2nd Italian campaign, once again demonstrating his bravery at the Battle of Marengo on 14th June 1800.

In 1804 he joined the *Chasseurs à cheval de la Garde Impériale*. During the years 1805 to 1807, Krettly took part in the campaigns in Austria, Prussia and Poland. During the Battle of Austerlitz he saved the life of one of his officers and took part in a charge against the Russian artillery, finishing the battle covered in sabre cuts. His bravery was rewarded with his being made second color bearer with the rank of second lieutenant in the regiment. At the Battle of Eylau, he contributed to the capture of a Russian battery of eighteen cannon and, at Friedland, his fearless behaviour led to him suffering serious wounds again. In recompense, Napoleon awarded him a life pension of 500 francs.

In 1808, incapable of continuing in active service due to the wounds received in so many years of fighting, he retired and was given the position of *garde-général des eaux et forêts* (general guard of waters and forests) in the calm locality of Montélimart. With the return of the Bourbons in 1814, he lost his position and was forced to flee to Belgium to avoid undergoing retaliation. He spent many years as a professor of music in Brussels until, in 1830, he returned to France. He obtained an appointment as a musician in the orchestra of the Gaiety Theatre, which he filled for ten years until his death in Paris on 16th January 1840.

Charles Parquin (1787-1845)

Charles Parquin enlisted in 1803, at the age of sixteen, in the *20e Chasseurs à cheval*, with whom he fought at Jena, Wagram, Fuentes de Oñoro and Salamanca where he was severely wounded. In February 1813, he was promoted to lieutenant and transferred to *13e Chasseurs à cheval.* Barely a month later, he transferred to the 10th Company of the *Chasseurs à cheval de la Garde Impériale*. Shortly after, he was promoted to Captain and transferred to the 11th Company. After participating in the 1814 campaign in France, he was witness to the melancholy farewell by Napoleon to his Imperial Guard at Fontainebleau.

Charles Parquin, author of famous memoirs and member of the *Chasseurs* of the Guard from 1813.

Although a valiant warrior, his greatest contribution to the saga of the Napoleonic Wars is his authorship of amusing and entertaining memoirs. These give clear evidence of his devotion to the Emperor and narrate details and anecdotes that allow us to know better the *Chasseurs à cheval de la Garde Impériale* during the final years of their existence.

François Lallemand (1774-1839)

He joined the *Guides* of the Army of Italy as a lieutenant in 1796 and was one of the squadron commanders of the *Chasseurs à cheval de la Garde Impériale* who remained faithful to Napoleon until his death. Following the Battle of Waterloo, Lallemand embarked on the British ship Bellerophon to accompany the Emperor and share his destiny. The British, however, would not allow him to follow Napoleon into exile on Saint Helena, considering him a fanatical supporter of the Emperor and, therefore, a source of unrest on the small island. After several years of captivity in England, he spent some months in Turkey and Egypt before arriving in the United States. Here he founded a colony in Texas where, with his brother Henri, they received hundreds of Bonapartist refugees. He also probably conspired to carry out an operation aimed at obtaining the liberation of Napoleon. However, when yellow fever decimated the inhabitants of the colony, it dissolved and Lallemand moved to Louisiana.

François Lallemand, one of the Emperor's more fanatical loyal squadron commanders.

In 1823 he returned Europe and was offered support to rise against the Bourbons in Spain. Before the failure of this revolt, Lallemand was transferred to Brussels, where he remained without money or friends. He then returned to the United States and worked for several years as a professor in New York. In 1830 he received the gratifying news that the Bourbons had been deposed and he returned to France, where he obtained a position in the Army High Command. He died nine years later in Paris from a heart attack.

Jean Baptiste Cavrois (1774-1820)

Cavrois enlisted as a private in 14th Line Infantry in 1791. Two years later, he transferred, with the rank of second lieutenant, to the 22e *Chasseurs à cheval*. He left this unit in 1802 to join the *Chasseurs à cheval* of the Consular Guard. Having fought with honour at the Battle of Austerlitz, he was promoted to the rank of squadron commander in 1805. He served with the *Chasseurs à cheval de la Garde Impériale* throughout the campaigns of 1806 and 1807 and then, in 1808, he became part of the Emperor's escort when he entered Spain. He left the Guard in 1809 to join the Army of Germany as commander of *20e Chasseurs à cheval*.

François Joseph Bohn (1763-1809)

Bohn enlisted in the 13th Regiment of Dragoons in 1785. Promoted on 10th April 1792, he campaigned with the Army of the North in 1792 and 1793, being wounded at the Battle of Neerwinden. He was promoted to second lieutenant on 12th April 1793 and transferred to the 1st Regiment of Hussars. With that unit and the rank of lieutenant, he participated in the campaigns of 1794 and 1795 with the Army of the Eastern Pyrenees. In 1797 he fought in Italy, where he awarded the rank of captain as a result of his valiant action in the Battle of San Marco, In this, while leading his Hussars, he managed to capture sixteen cannon, thirty limbers, seven standards and 5,000 prisoners.

On 18th August 1802, Bohn was transferred, with his captain's rank, to the elite regiment of the *Chasseurs à cheval de la Garde*. In 1804 he became a regimental squadron commander. The following year he participated in the glorious charge of the *Chasseurs* at Austerlitz. In 1806 and 1807 he fought in Germany and Poland and, in 1808, was sent to Spain.

His involvement with the *Chasseurs à cheval de la Garde* ended on 16th March 1809, when he was named Colonel of 7e *Chasseurs à cheval*. He was killed, on 14th June 1809, at the Battle of Raab (Hungary) while leading his new command.

Chasseur of the Guard during the 1808 Campaign. This *Chasseur* appears to be demanding that the unfortunate farmer give him the requisitioned forage he needs for the horses. Not even an elite unit like the *Chasseurs* escaped the extreme rigours of campaign life. During this particular campaign, the commander of the *Chasseurs*, Lefèbvre-Desnoëttes, ordered them to wear a scarlet plume. However, in this magnificent painting, the artist, unfortunately, represents it as a green one. (Watercolor by Hippolyte Lecomte, Anne S. K. Brown Collection).

ON CAMPAIGN

THE GUIDES IN THE FIRST ITALIAN CAMPAIGN (1796-1797)

Lonato

Two months after its creation, the company of *Guides* of the Army of Italy received its baptism of fire at the battle of Lonato, fought on 3rd August 1796. In this combat, twenty-five *Guides* charged, in company with the 15th Regiment of Dragoons, to assist General Masséna's troops who were being hard pressed by the Austrians under the command of General Quasdanovitch. The charge led by Napoleon's aide-de-camp Junot, known as "The Tempest"; became an unstoppable tide that succeeded in relieving Masséna's vanguard of which the Austrians had taken prisoner a regiment of Hussars. Later, the *Guides* and Dragoons fought with the regiment of Uhlans of Benda. Junot, in spite of receiving several sabre cuts, fought like a lion and did not cease encouraging his men, who ended up dispersing the Uhlans. The intervention of Guyeaux's infantry division caused the battle to be decided in favour of the French.

Roveredo

In September 1796, Bonaparte continued his triumphal advance across the Italian

▲ The Battle of Austerlitz. Prince Repnine, who was taken prisoner, is paraded, together with a number of captured standards, before Napoleon by General Rapp. (Oil on canvas by François Gerard).

▲ Prince Repnine in the uniform of the Cavalier Gardai (Courtesy of Michel Repnine).

Guide of the Eastern Army. Mounted on an Arab horse with an Eastern-style harness and wearing a djellaba as protection against the desert sand and sun. He is equipped with a Model 1776 light cavalry sabre. The chevrons on the bicorne are white instead of the usual *aurore*, and indicate that he is an auxiliary *Guide*. This unit, composed of 1,244 men, constituted a reserve for the army in Egypt and was first manifestation of the idea of creating a body like the Consular, later Imperial Guard. (Illustration by D. A. C.).

peninsular. In Roveredo he fought, on 4th of that month, a further battle against the Austrians. At a particular point in the battle, Bonaparte launched a charge of a brigade of Colonel Dubois' Hussars; the Colonel fell mortally wounded after being hit three times. At this point, the charge lost momentum before the Austrian cavalry. Following this failure, Bessières was given the order to charge at the head of the *Guides* and rectify the situation. The remainder of the French army, inspired by the bravery shown by the *Guides*, followed its example and the battle finished with more than 4,000 Austrian prisoners. That same afternoon, Bessières was promoted squadron commander.

Bassano

Two days after Roveredo the French surrounded the retiring Austrians. A dozen *Guides* under the command of lieutenant Guérin was sent against the Croatian infantry battalions' rearguard covering the retirement. It was during this engagement, ending with the surrender of the Croatians, that *maréchal-des-logis* Hercules and Bonnet, the trumpeter, distinguished themselves.

The *Guides* of the Commander-in-Chief of the Army of Italy in 1796. The bicorne and green dress coat *"à la chasseur"* were the distinguishing features of Bonaparte's *Guides*. (Illustration by D. A. C.).

Arcole

In November 1796, a new Austrian army under the command of General Alvintzi threatened the situation of the French in Italy. During the Battle of Arcole, Bonaparte requested that Bessières select an especially energetic, brave *Guide* to put at the head of twenty-five *Guides* and several trumpeters. Hercules was the one selected, and he crossed some marshland, charged the enemy left while raising such a cacophony of sound with his trumpets that the Austrians retired, thinking that they were being attacked by a powerful force of cavalry.

Rivoli and La Favorita

On 14th January 1797, the *Guides,* under the command of Bessières, continued to enhance their brilliant performance throughout the Italian campaign, including the charges across the Rivoli plateau together with 200 hussars led by Lasalle. These charges were key to the French victory, since they prevented the conjunction of two Austrian forces that, united, would have been very difficult to beat. Two days later, in the combat of La Favorita, a joint attack of *Guides* and the brigade of infantry under the command of General Victor broke the Austrian line completely. The Austrian defeat caused the surrender of General Provera and the fall of the fortress of Mantua.

Bonaparte showed his admiration and gratitude towards the *Guides* by sending Bessières to Paris with the captured standards and a letter

▲ Battle of Mount Tabor, 16th April 1799. On the Plain of Esdrelon, in the same location where King Saul fought the Philistines and Josiah fought the Egyptians, Bonaparte's *Guides* fought with fury against the Mamelukes. (Oil on canvas by Louis François Lejeune).

addressed to the members of the Directory that said:

"Citizen Directors: I send you eleven standards captured from the Austrians at the battles of Rivoli and La Favorita. Citizen Bessières, commander of the *Guides*, the carrier of this letter, is an officer who has distinguished himself by his bravery and by the honour which he has enjoyed when commanding a group of valiant men which he has not hesitated to bring into battle against the enemy cavalry, rendering the most signal service."

THE GUIDES IN EGYPT (1798-1799)

The Revolt of Cairo

Bonaparte disembarked in Egypt in 1798, accompanied by his *Guides*. Despite the victories gained in the following months at Alexandria and The Pyramids, the rebellious native population remained determined to resist to the invader. On 21st October, the streets of Cairo exploded in rebellion and two hundred French soldiers of the garrison were assassinated. As soon as Bonaparte received news of the revolt, he set out for the capital escorted by his *Guides*. At dawn on 22nd, Bonaparte's *aide-de-camp*, *chef-de-brigade* Sukolwski, was given the order to advance on the centre of the city, still in French hands, with fifteen *Guides*. They were all caught and massacred by the insurgents and their bodies thrown to the wild dogs. That same day, *maréchal-des-logis* Charroy and four *Guides à cheval* were sent with a message to the post commanded by General Verdier. The five valiant *Guides* succeeded in getting out of Cairo under a hail of bullets, crossing a district controlled by the insurgents. On the way they had to charge against a group of Turkish horsemen, whom they defeated, allowing them to complete their mission successfully.

The Passage of the Red Sea

At the end of 1798, Bonaparte set out to explore the Isthmus of Suez to verify for himself what possibilities existed to construct a channel that would connect the Mediterranean to the Red Sea. Throughout this expedition a company of Guides, commanded by squadron commander Barthélemy, escorted him. One day, Bonaparte and his *Guides*, accompanied by officials of the General Staff, traversed waters over a tongue of land revealed by the low tide. After visiting the Spring of Moses, the expedition decided to return to camp, but the high tide and the darkness prevented their finding the way back. Desperate, the group finally thought that it could cross the deep waters on the backs of their horses. In spite of proceeding with extreme caution, General Caffarelli fell into the water. *Guide* Louis was sent to the rescue of the General, who was unable to swim because of his wooden leg. He saved the General and, after a superhuman effort, the *Guides* succeeded in leading the party to safety on the other shore. *Guide* Louis received a Sabre of Honour with the legend *Le Général Bonaparte au guide à cheval Louis* on one face of the blade and, on the other, *Passage de la Mer Rouge*.

▲ *Guides* of the Eastern Army at Mount Tabor, 1799. This illustration drawn done taking as models the *Guides* represented in the picture by Lejeune of the Battle of Mount Tabor. The *Guides* have raised the edge of their *schabraques* to be able to readily gain access to their pistols. Two figures wear *colbacks* while another wears a bicorne as it is not known for sure what headdress they wore during this campaign. (Illustration by M. Benigni according to the painting by Lejeune. The Author's collection).

Mount Tabor

The battle of Mount Tabor was fought on the 16th April 1799. During the battle, Bessières, commanding four squadrons of *Guides à cheval*, charged against the Mamelukes. This action was decisive in securing a victory of 6,000 French over 25,000 Turks.

St John of Acre

Following the Battle of Mount Tabor, Bonaparte returned to resume siege operations against the fortress of St John of Acre. In the final assault against the walls, the *Guides* left their horses and fought alongside the infantry. Thirty-nine of them died in the breach, with double this number wounded.

Detail of the *Guides* of the Eastern Army taken from a picture of the Battle of Mount Tabor by Lejeune. Although the artist represents the *Guides* wearing the *colback*, it is more likely that they wore bicornes. ▼

Aboukir

During the Battle of Aboukir, fought on 25th April 1799, the *Guides* wrote one of the most illustrious pages of their history. On that day, a new Turkish army, including 18,000 Janissaries, supported by powerful artillery plus some British forces, disembarked in Aboukir Bay, between the sea and Lake Madieh, where they established two solid lines of redoubts. Bonaparte, although he only had 7,000 men, did not delay in

▲ Battle of Marengo, 14th June 1800. During this battle, the company of *Chasseurs* of the Consular Guard lost seventy horses of the 115 it had at the beginning of the day, which gives a clear idea of the ferocity of the fighting in which these men were engaged. (Oil on canvas by Louis François Lejeune).

▶ Detail of Lejeune's painting of the Battle of Marengo. The aide-de-camp stands out from the others due to his sky blue uniform. To his left is Beauharnais.

attacking. The *Guides* were sent into the attack to reinforce Murat's four hundred sabres, which, after their first charge, were forced to retire. The already famous Captain Hercules was awarded a battlefield promotion to squadron commander after the battle. On his own initiative, he assaulted the redoubts until the French infantry approached them frontally, causing the enemy to retreat. When *Napoleon* reprimanded him for having left the body of his formation to carry out a mission that nobody had entrusted to him, the valiant black merely shrugged his shoulders and retorted: "What do you want me to say, my general? Everything has turned out well".

THE SECOND ITALIAN CAMPAIGN (1800)

Marengo

At the beginning of May 1800, the company of *Chasseurs à cheval* of the Consular Guard left Paris to take part in the second Italian campaign. Bonaparte crossed the St Bernard Pass in the Alps, escorted by his faithful Guard which, on this expedition, would only become involved in combat at the Battle of Marengo, fought on 14th June. After a difficult engagement with Austrian cavalry under the command of the Prince of Lichtenstein, of the 115 *Chasseurs à cheval* who started the battle, there were just forty-five effectives left at the end of the day. At Marengo, men like second lieutenant Daumesnil, who captured an Austrian Dragoon general, stood out. Also, *brigadier-trompette* Krettly, when acting as Bonaparte's escort, saw an Austrian battery firing on the group and charged with a few *Chasseurs*, capturing two cannon –an action that won him a *trompette d'honneur*. Furthermore, *Maréchal-des-logis* Rabusson, with four *Chasseurs*, out-faced twelve Austrian Dragoons, making them flee and capturing the officer in command of the group. Young Eugène Beauharnais, commanding the *Chasseurs à cheval*, deserved these words contained in a letter written by Bonaparte to Josephine, Eugène's mother: "Your son advances quickly towards posterity. He has covered himself with glory in the actions that we have carried out in Italy; he will become one of the greatest captains in Europe".

▲
Squadron Commander Beauharnais at the Battle of Marengo. The equipment and some elements of the uniform worn by Beauharnais are a complete fantasy. The standard sabre and bridle have been replaced with a scimitar and an extremely elaborate Hungarian bridle. The *schabraque* of panther skin is shown with the tail lying across the horse's hindquarters, instead of the other way round. He wears riding breeches, or *charivari*, instead of scarlet trousers. The bandolier is shown as red leather instead of the prescribed green. Finally, the *colback* is shown decorated with cords - highly unusual. (Illustration by M. Benigni from a painting by Lejeune. The Author's collection).

1805
Ulm

The first days of the French advance through central Germany, from the Rhine to the Danube, saw General Mack's 40,000 Austrians surrounded in Ulm and their communications with Vienna and the Russian armies of Czar Alexander cut. The *Chasseurs à cheval de la Garde* remained with the Emperor, entering Augsburg with him on 13th October. At dusk on the 14th they were in Albeck, from where the walls of Ulm were already visible. On 15th, the famous La Tour dragoon regiment left Ulm to attack Ney's troops, who struggled to cross the Elchingen bridge, to the north of the Danube, to complete the encirclement of the city. Bessières, seeing the threat that was hanging over Ney's men, sent the *Chasseurs à cheval*, the Grenadiers and the Mamelukes of the Guard to face the Austrian Dragoons. In a terrible storm that inundated the land and through which the horses advanced with extreme difficulty, a hand-to-hand mêlée was fought in which single riders could strike one another only with their sabres' hand guards, given the impossibility of executing cuts or thrusts in such a large mass of riders fighting as if in a street fight. During that chaotic encounter, the La Tour regiment demonstrated that its reputation was no myth and put up a ferocious resistance but, eventually, the Austrian horsemen were themselves forced to retire towards Ulm.

That night, the exhausted *Chasseurs* took refuge in buildings constructed to lodge members of the Imperial household. When they had settled in, numerous servants of the Emperor appeared, who were violently expelled. The episode came to Napoleon's attention and the *Chasseurs* found themselves outdoors again, in the cold and the mud.

On the night of 14th to 15th October, Napoleon ordered Murat to reunite all the cavalry that had been used at Ulm and use them to pursue the Austrian force located to the north of the Danube. As punishment for their previous audacity, the *Chasseurs* were placed in the van of this pursuit with the result that, for ten days, they were denied the privilege of escorting the Emperor. This infuriated them and spurred them to fight like men

Officer of *the Cavalier Gardai* charging at Austerlitz (Illustration by V. N. Konnov).

Soldier of the Preobrazhenski Regiment. During the Battle of Austerlitz, the heavy fire of the Russians from the Preobrazhenski was the cause of the death of *Major* Morland as well as other notable losses amongst the *Chasseurs* of the Imperial Guard. (Illustration of D. A. C.).

possessed alongside the other regiments under Murat's command. In five days of constant fighting and after covering about 200 kilometres in extreme weather conditions, the French cavalry captured eighteen generals, 12,500 men, eleven standards, 120 guns and more than 1,500 ammunition wagons and provisions. On 21st October, Murat wrote to Napoleon: "This afternoon, the remainder of Prince Ferdinand's army have been beaten on the highway that goes from Nuremberg to Fürth. I must emphasize the excellent behaviour of the cavalry and, especially, of the *Chasseurs à cheval* of your Guard, who began the attack and overpowered the enemy cavalry in spite of being very inferior in number". On the 29th the *Chasseurs* met again with their beloved Emperor, who expressed his satisfaction with their valiant behaviour during the pursuit of the Austrians. Previous infractions were pardoned and the *Chasseurs* returned to their position of honour as escorts to Napoleon.

Austerlitz

At around 11.00 in the morning of 2nd December 1805, the Battle of Austerlitz was at its height. A bayonet attack by the Russian Guard infantry had penetrated the front line of Vandamme's division, but the fire of the second line forced the Russians to retire. Then, following an order from Napoleon, Vandamme began to advance his division by the right flank, a movement that exposed its left flank and rear. Grand Duke Constantine, in command of the Russian Imperial Guard cavalry, became aware of the opportunity offered and sent his squadrons of Cuirassiers and Hussars against the French General, striking at the point where the infantry, who had been forced to retire, were reorganizing.

Vandamme attempted to repulse the enemy attack, ordering *4e Ligne* and *24e Légère* to move towards its left to face the great mass of cavalry that were approaching. Two battalions of the 4e were swept away, one of them losing its Eagle and most of its men their arms. The impetus of the Russian cavalry charge carried them into the lines of Drouet d'Erlon's division, which had advanced in support of Vandamme. Napoleon, who was close by, witnessed the chaos in the infantry lines, and ordered Bessières to remedy the disastrous situation.

Soldier of *the Cavalier Gardai* (Illustration by D. A. C.).

First, Bessières ordered Morland, the colonel of the *Chasseurs à cheval de la Garde Impériale*, with two

of his squadrons to go to the rescue of the survivors of *4e Ligne*, who had been taken prisoner by the Russian grenadiers. The Russian cavalry had retired before the infantry, in the middle of which was a square formed by the Semienovski Guard regiment. The attack by both squadrons of *Chasseurs* in line dispersed the Russian infantry and arrived in front of this square. Immediately, the *Chasseurs* were, themselves, harassed by a sharp fusillade from the Preobrazhenski regiment whom they encountered amongst some nearby vines. Morland was mortally wounded, but, assisted by two of his *Chasseurs*, he was able to stay on his horse and return to the French ranks with some difficulty.

Bessières realized that something more powerful would be required to end the obstinate resistance of the Russian infantry. Leaving two squadrons, one of *Chasseurs à cheval de la Garde Impériale* and another of *Grenadiers à cheval de la Garde Impériale,* with the Emperor, he placed himself at the front of a force the front rank of which was formed by the other three squadrons of *Chasseurs*, now under the command of Colonel Dahlmann, together with the company of Mamelukes. The second line comprised three squadrons of *Grenadiers à cheval*, supported by two batteries of the Guard Artillery. Napoleon's veteran aide-de-camp, General Jean Rapp, took command of the Mamelukes. This time, the charge of the French Imperial Guard cavalry swept aside the Semienovski Guards and then confronted the Russian Imperial Guard cavalry, the Cuirassiers and Hussars, and a tremendous mêlée took place that ended with the defeat and death of many Russian cavalrymen.

Spurred on by the success of the

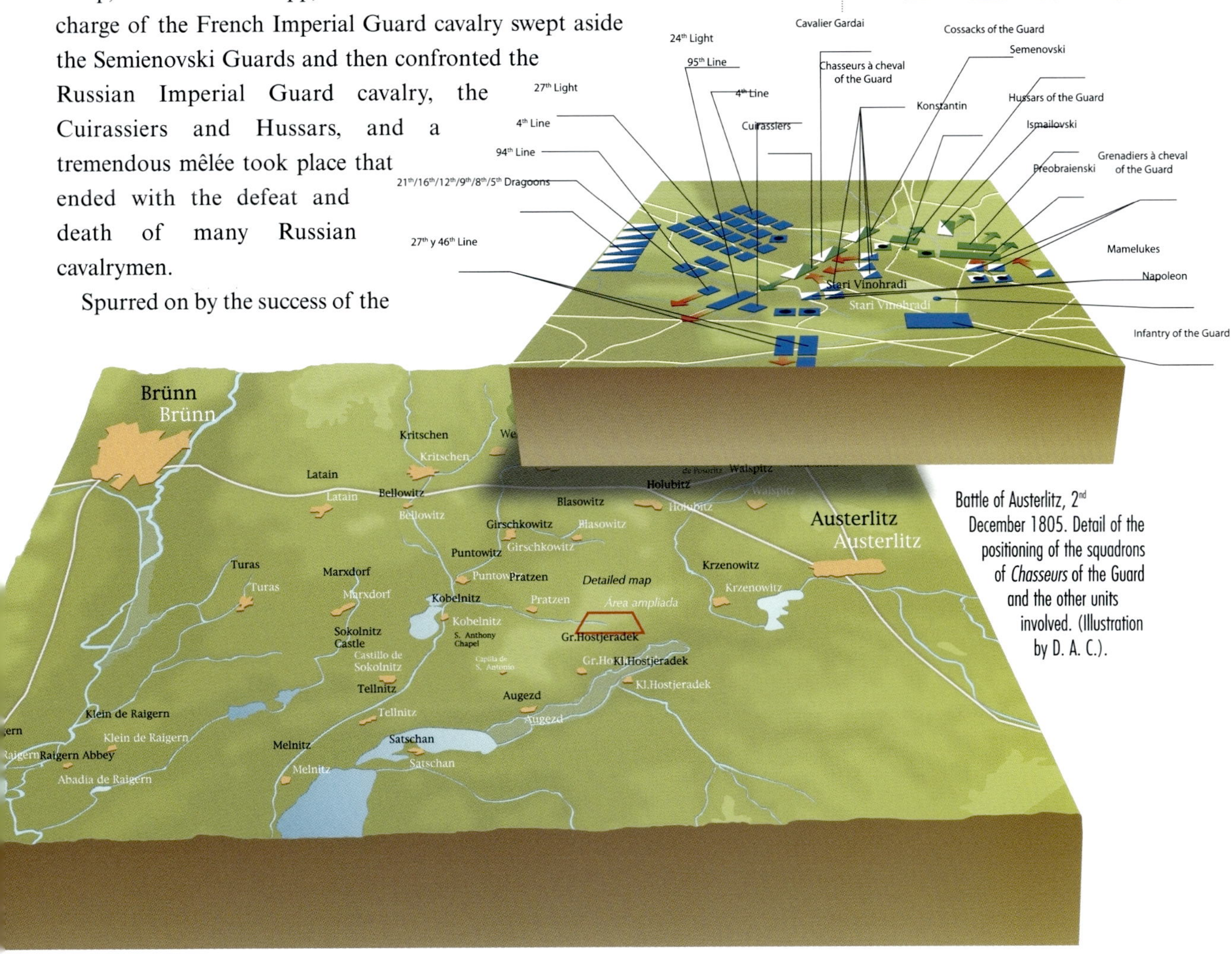

Battle of Austerlitz, 2nd December 1805. Detail of the positioning of the squadrons of *Chasseurs* of the Guard and the other units involved. (Illustration by D. A. C.).

The *Chasseurs* of the Guard charging against the Russian Imperial Guard cavalry at the Battle of Austerlitz. Heading the *chasseurs* at the charge is Daumesnil, the Squadron Commander. Beside him are a *brigadier* and *a maréchal des logis*. At Austerlitz, the *Chasseurs* wore pelisses and the '*à la mandrin*" cape, that is to say rolled and slung across the right shoulder for protection against sabre cuts. The *schabraque* was decorated with a hunting horn. It was not until 1806 that this was replaced with the Imperial Eagle. The carbines are positioned with the muzzle outside their leather boot so it could be brought into use faster. (Illustration by D.A.C.).

▶ *Chasseurs* of the Guard charging during the campaign in France, 1814. (Watercolor by L. Rousselot, Anne S. K. Brown Collection).

first charge and, after reuniting with the French cavalry who had been dispersed after the violent shock, Rapp decided to attack the Russian infantry and artillery. However, this time, a formidable obstacle appeared before him: eight squadrons of the *Cavalier Gardai* and Cossacks of the Imperial Russian Guard, who had appeared on the scene to assist their comrades. The shock between these two elite units was extremely violent and ended with a series of one-on-one duels across the length and breadth of the plain and the valley between the Pratzen Heights and Krzenowitz, towards the east. Rapp found himself surrounded by a group of Russian riders who invited him to surrender. Despite being injured by two sabre cuts, Rapp was prepared to sell his life dearly. However, just in time, a group of Guard *Chasseurs*, commanded by Captain Daumesnil, appeared and routed the surprised Russians.

Finally, the valour and determination of the French cavalry managed to defeat the *Cavalier Gardai*. Their commander, young Prince Repnine, 200 of their noble horsemen and several standards were captured and taken before Napoleon by the fortunate Rapp, who proudly displayed the cuts that the Russian sabres had made in his dress coat.

Mameluke. A company of Mamelukes, riders from as far a field as Arabia, Greece and the Caucasus, they were assigned to the *Chasseurs à Cheval* of the Imperial Guard from July 1804. *Chasseurs* and Mamelukes charged together at the Battle of Austerlitz. They also found themselves surrounded during the Madrid uprising of 2nd May 1808. (Henschell Collection. Kunstbibliothek, Berlin). ▼

1806

During 1806, the *Chasseurs* took no part in the Battle of Jena. Because of Napoleon's rapid strategic movements, they had been left far behind. During that period, the responsibility as the Emperor's escort fell on the 1st Hussars. However, by the time of Napoleon's triumphal entrance into Berlin, the *Chasseurs à cheval de la Garde Impériale* had once again taken up its position of honour.

1807

On 8th February 1807 the *Chasseurs à cheval de la Garde Impériale* would again be involved in fighting, this time on the frozen fields of Eylau. The regiment took part in the massive charge of eighty squadrons of cavalry, under the command of Murat, which saved the French centre from pressure exerted by the Russians. Unfortunately, the regiment's losses were grave, among them Nicolas Dahlmann, the Colonel of the *Chasseurs*. On that day, the *Chasseurs* lost 21 officers and 224 men, killed or wounded.

1808

Madrid

On 2nd May 1808, the *Chasseurs à cheval de la Garde Impériale* were quartered in the convent of San Francisco, in the district of the Buen Retiro, at the far end of the city from the Royal Palace, when the popular uprising began that signalled the start of Spanish resistance against Napoleon. Pierre Daumesnil, in command of the squadron, issued the order to his men to mount up, cross the city and join Murat's forces. As soon as they left their quarters they rode into what can

only be described as hell. They were fired on from windows, and had water and boiling oil poured on them but, in spite of this, they managed to make their way to headquarters. It had not been the kind of heroic situation to which these men were accustomed. Then, a few hours later, they received the order to break through again and escort squadron commander Rossetii, one of Murat's *aides-de-camp*, who had to take a message to General Gobert. The General was with his division on the Retiro, on the other side of the city. Daumesnil, leading 300 *Chasseurs* and Mamelukes, set off at the gallop, while the bells of Madrid tolled dismally. In the Puerta del Sol, they were set upon by an angry mob; women even tried to throw themselves at the horses' hindquarters to stab them and attempt to dismount the riders. Daumesnil miraculously survived and managed to escape, with his men, a slaughter that had little to do with the glorious actions of the likes of Austerlitz or Eylau.

THE CAVALRY CHARGE

The French cavalry regulations, which followed the principles of Frederick the Great like the cavalry manuals of the rest of the European armies, established the following successive events for a charge:

The cavalry – that probably commenced in a static position – received the order to attack. Sabres were pulled from their scabbards and placed on the shoulder and the riders advanced to toward the enemy in two lines.

After advancing forty paces (25 metres), the order was given to advance at the trot. The riders had to advance in silence to be able to hear the words of command above the tumult of battle. The officers issued the orders and the front line followed the pace and direction marked by the officers who went in front.

The trot continued until arriving within about 100 metres of the enemy. At that point, the commanding officer increased the pace to the canter, during which the lines still remained in order, with the riders knee-to-knee.

When 50 meters from the enemy, the commanding officer ordered the trumpeters to sound the charge. The horsemen gave spur and galloped towards the enemy piercing their lines. This charge was called *"charge la sauvage"*. The horsemen braced themselves in their stirrups and relaxed the reins. Those in the front rank pointed their sabre-tips forwards and those in the second rank raised them over their heads. At this moment, they shouted *"Avancez!"*

In the final 50 metres, the officers who were at the front reduced speed so that the front rank could catch up with them. By this method they avoided being isolated and becoming an easy target at short range. The officers, or sergeant-majors who had ridden behind the formation to prevent anybody attempting to abscond during the charge, spurred their horses forward to reach the second line and join the mêlée.

▲
The Battle of Somosierra. This battle, fought on 30th November 1808, opened the gates of Madrid to Napoleon. (Oil on canvas by François Lejeune).

Somosierra

On 30th November 1808 the Guard *Chasseurs* took part in the cavalry charge that cleared the passage of the Somosierra Pass and the subsequent entry of Napoleon into Madrid. They suffered hardly any losses since, in the first charge they were in support of 3rd Polish squadron of the 1st regiment of *Chevau-Légers*. The lancers, on the other hand, were particularly hard hit by musket fire from the Spanish infantry. In a second charge, carried out with the support of the infantry, the Poles and the *Chasseurs* completely routed the Spanish artillerymen and infantry.

Benavente

On 29th December 1808, after crossing the Guadarrama Pass in a blizzard, Napoleon was in pursuit of the British Expeditionary Army, sent to the Iberian Peninsula under Sir John Moore, to support the Spanish uprising. Before the French numerical superiority, the British were forced to retire on Corunna, where they would embark their troops in order to return home. In the meantime, however, they still had time to cause serious damage to Napoleon, capturing one of his more famous generals: Lefèbvre-Desnöettes. Ambushed by the 10th Hussars, pickets of the 18th Hussars and the 3rd Hussars of the King's German Legion, the *Chasseurs à cheval de la Garde Impériale* were surrounded while fording the Esla River at Benavente. The regiment's colonel, General Lefèbvre-Desnöettes, was wounded by a pistol ball and captured by Private Levi Grisdale, of the 10th Hussars. In addition, six further officers were wounded and two captains captured while fifty-five *Chasseurs* were captured with a further seventy-three killed or wounded. The sojourn in

Spain was never to be a pleasant memory for the *Chasseurs* or, over the course of years, for the Emperor. It was just days after the debacle at Benavente that Napoleon quit the Peninsula with his *enfants chéris* and set off fort Austria.

▲ An officer in the uniform of an *aide-de-camp* and a lieutenant in campaign dress. The lieutenant, mounted on a chestnut horse, wears the troopers' campaign uniform: *colback* without cords or plume, *charivari* or riding breeches instead of Hungarian trousers and *sabretache* with cover. In the 1808 Spanish Campaign, the *colback* plume was totally scarlet instead of green with a scarlet tip, so this indicates that the wearer is an aide-de-camp. (Illustration by M. Benigni. The Author's collection).

1809

At the Battle of Wagram, fought between 5th and 6th July 1809, the regiment of *Chasseurs à cheval de la Garde Impériale*, together with the remainder of the Guard cavalry, supported the right flank of Macdonald's great column that would deliver the decisive blow that would gain a French victory. Four officers and twenty *Chasseurs* were killed. Majors Daumesnil and Corbineau were wounded and each lost a leg.

1810 AND 1811.

In March 1810, the *Chasseurs à cheval de la Garde Impériale* returned to Spain as part of the Army of the North commanded by General Dorsenne. In November of that year, at Lerma, about 150 *Chasseurs* carried out an action against a party of guerrillas of Cura Merino.

In May of the following year, about 300 *Chasseurs* took part in the battle of Fuentes de Oñoro, as part of the Imperial Guard cavalry under the command of Bessières. The prudence of their Commander-in-Chief meant they took little part in the battle. The *Chasseurs* again left the Peninsula in March 1812 without managing to add any further laurels to the history of the regiment.

1812

Five squadrons of *Chasseurs à cheval de la Garde Impériale* and the company of Mamelukes took part in the Russian campaign. However, they took no part in the battles of Smolensk and Borodino; Napoleon did not want to risk the last reserve of his army when so far from France. An incident worthy of mention happened at Malojaroslavetz, during the retreat very early on the day after the battle, Napoleon, wishing to view the battlefield, left with a detachment of Polish lancers who mistook a group of Cossacks for French cavalry. Recognizing the danger, General Armand Caulaincourt, Duke of Vicenza, escorted Napoleon off the road and led a squadron of *Chasseurs* in a charge against the Cossacks. As soon as Bessières realised the danger the Emperor was in, he rode to his rescue with squadrons of *Grenadiers à cheval*, Dragoons and *Chasseurs*. Nine *Chasseurs* gave their lives for Napoleon that day with a further seven wounded.

Detail of the picture by Lejeune of the Battle of Somosierra. ▼

1813

In 1813, the regiment suffered the loss of twenty-six officers, seven of them at the Battle of Leipzig, fought on 18th October. At the end of the year, the Old Guard, commanded by General Lion,

A *Chasseur* of the Imperial Guard during the 1812 Russian campaign. This *Chasseur*, without much success, attempts to use his dolman to protect himself against the bitter cold. He has three length-of-service chevrons that indicate he has twenty years service and he has covered his *sabretache* with a waxed fabric cover. He has tied the tail of his chestnut horse to avoid stains from the mud and snow otherwise the swishing of the tail would splash his uniform. (Illustration by M. Benigni. The Author's collection).

and the squadrons of the Young Guard commanded by Colonel Meuziau, separated. The former remained with the *Grande Armée*, while the latter marched to Belgium, where they participated in the defence of Antwerp under the command of Lefèbvre-Desnöettes.

1814

With the borders of France under threat, the regiment fought bravely throughout the 1814 campaign. The most outstanding episode was the charge of Kirmann's squadron at St. Dizier on the 20th March. Having been given the order to charge eighteen Russian guns firing deadly case shot, Kirmann obeyed without hesitation. With the support of the Red Lancers, the *Chasseurs* captured the enemy guns. The Emperor was informed of the action by General Sebastiani saying, "I have been a cavalry officer for twenty-five years, and I have never seen a more brilliant charge than that carried out by the squadron that went in at the front".

1815

Waterloo would be the last battle for the soldiers of the Emperor. In this final combat, the *Chasseurs* of the Old Guard, led by Lefèbvre Desnoëttes, were the point of the spear of the second big wave of cavalry charges against Wellington's positions located between La Haye Sainte and Hougoumont. When the French realised the battle was about to be lost, Lefèbvre Desnoëttes, whose Bonapartist fanaticism would not allow him to accept defeat, began to attack desperately. He sought death on the battlefield but, in spite of his desire, he was merely wounded. Twenty officers fell, six of whom subsequently died. The testimony of a British officer speaks of the desire, on the part of the *Chasseur* officers, to fight to the last man, and it reveals the pragmatism of the British soldier against the romantic search for death by a soldier of Napoleon's Guard: "Time and time again, some of the squadrons of *Chasseurs* advanced towards us to challenge the officers of our regiment to single combat. As they were a much stronger regiment, I could not accept such an honour... "

THE EMPEROR'S ESCORT

▲ Passage of the Guadarrama (end of November / beginning of December 1808). Another hard trial confronting the Chasseurs of the Guard in Spain: escorting the Emperor during the passage, in mid-winter, of the Guadarrama Pass. (Oil on canvas by Hippolyte Bellangé).

Napoleon always remembered the passage of the Bridge of Arcola on 17th November 1796 as one of the moments when his life had been in the greatest danger. At the head of his troops, he attempted to cross the difficult passage whilst opposed by tenacious resistance from the Austrians. The confusion caused by an enemy counterattack ended with his falling into the water. Napoleon, submerged up to his shoulders in dark, marshy mud and with bullets flying over his head, thought that his end had come. Luckily, his brother Louis, who had been impotently observing the scene, rescued him with the aid of a young officer named Auguste Marmont. However, this was far from the only occasion when Napoleon diced with death. During the siege of Toulon, three years earlier, an English bayonet had caused a dangerous wound and, throughout the following twenty-two years, although he was never again wounded, he had eighteen horses killed under him on the battlefield.

Napoleon also survived many assassination attempts. During the *coup d'état* of 18e Brumaire (November 1799) a member of the Council of Five Hundred attempted to stab him. A grenadier of Napoleon's escort, however, prevented the would-be assassin, from administering the fatal blow. In September 1800, an attack on Napoleon was frustrated by a miracle at the Paris Opera. Then, on Christmas Eve of that same year, conspirators loyal to the Bourbons placed a loaded powder barrel on the carriageway, causing a terrible

▲
Chasseurs à Cheval on escort duty on foot. As they are wearing the uniform '*à chasseur*' on escort duty, it is safe to assume that the scene takes place during the Polish Campaign of 1807 (Vinkhuijzen Collection of Military Uniforms, NYPL).

explosion that dismounted some of the Grenadiers of the Consular Guard escort and caused the death of several civilians, including a girl.

Napoleon, once he became France's military and political leader, made many enemies both on and off the battlefield. This was the primary reason why his troops of the Guard, first Consular, and then Imperial - men who were much more than simple escorts and would become inseparable comrades - vowed to protect the life of the person whom they admired so much.

On campaign, Napoleon always had, close by, four squadrons of the different units of the *Chasseurs à cheval de la Garde Impériale*, Polish Lancers, Empress Dragoons or Horse Grenadiers, who would attack any enemy if the Emperor were in the slightest danger. To the *Chasseurs à cheval* squadron - more frequently called "*Guides à cheval* " when they undertook such escort work - he entrusted them with clearly defined tasks. Two units comprising a lieutenant, a sergeant, two corporals, twenty-two *Chasseurs* and a trumpeter rode ahead and behind the Emperor. A corporal and four *Chasseurs* formed an advance party and cleared the way for the retinue. One of the *Chasseurs*, the *Chasseur de portefeuille*, was responsible for the leather bag containing the Emperor's military equipment, maps and telescope. If Napoleon stopped and dismounted, the *chasseurs* followed suit, fixed bayonets to their carbines and formed an outward facing square with the Emperor in the centre. The officer in command of the escort was beside him at all times. Only Murat and the Prince of Neuchâtel had precedence over this officer.

Wherever the Emperor lodged, this officer occupied the adjoining room. The escorting *Chasseurs* dismounted and remained on foot opposite the Imperial lodging, standing guard. Immediately outside the door was a ready-saddled horse, held by one of the team of young men, in readiness for any need to flee. These men were relieved every two hours to maintain alertness day or night. The first person whom the Emperor saw when leaving his room was the officer commanding the escort. This position was thus a great responsibility, but also a great honour. This group of men was totally faithful to Napoleon, deserving a substantial reward for their fidelity. In each company, there were four *Chasseurs* who received not only the Legion of Honour and the Cross of the Iron Crown with their salary of 250 francs, but also an extra income of between 500 and 800 francs.

During the Polish campaign of 1807, an insignificant episode occurred, but which offers a vivid image of the relationship between the Emperor and the *Chasseurs* in charge of his protection. During each and every one of the days that that campaign lasted, Napoleon mounted his horse before dawn and rode to inspect the advance posts, followed by the squadron that served him as escort. Before noon, Napoleon dismounted, and the *Chasseurs* lit a great fire and prepared a refuge of straw and branches for him. In that makeshift

THE CHERISHED CHILDREN

Napoleon, conscious of the devotion that his *Chasseurs à Cheval* felt for him, often allowed them comments that would certainly never have been tolerated from mouths that were not those of his "cherished children". One day, the horse of one of the *Chasseurs* who preceded Napoleon fell, with its rider. The *Chasseur* was fighting to regain his saddle when the Emperor happened in front of him and called him "clumsy". Shortly after, the Emperor's horse fell to the ground in a cloud of dust. The *Chasseur* had remounted his horse and returned to occupy his position in the vanguard. When he happened later to be next to the Emperor, he shouted sufficiently loudly to be heard by Napoleon: "it seems that I am not the only clumsy one on the road today".

"cottage" he received intelligence and distributed new orders. While his personal Mameluke, Roustan, prepared lunch for him, the *Chasseurs*, with fixed bayonets, formed a circle around the camp that nobody could penetrate. One day, during this lunch break, Napoleon approached a *Vélite* who was in front of him and asked:

– 'Who has appointed you to my Guard?'

– 'You have, Your Majesty', answered Guyot Desherbiers, the *Vélite*

– 'Explain yourself, I do not understand you'

– 'Sire, I have reached this position thanks to Your Majesty's decree which allows young people of rich families to join the Guard if they fulfil the conditions imposed.'

– 'You are too short', said Napoleon, shaking his head.

– 'Sire, I serve as well as the biggest in my regiment'.

– 'You have been under enemy fire?'.

– 'Yes, Sire, I was at the passage of the Bug'.

– 'It was a hard fight! You surely were afraid... I see that you blush and you do not answer me, I must have guessed right'.

– 'Yes, Sire, I recognize that I was afraid but it only lasted a little while'.

– 'Console yourself, then. There are many others who were afraid and for whom it lasted longer. You are a good soldier. You will have lunch with me, does that please you?'

– 'Certainly, Sire!' The *Vélite* exclaimed, overcome at being the recipient of such an honour.

Napoleon on campaign. Young *vélites* of the Guard. *Vélite* Desherbiers eats lunch with Napoleon while the rest of the Chasseurs remain alert to guarantee the Emperor's safety. (Engraving by H. Bellangé. The Author's collection).

Then, leaving his carbine behind him, the young *Vélite* sat next to the Emperor. Soon, Roustan, with the same respect as if he was serving a general, offered the man a small platter of silver containing some slices of ham. Desherbiers ate with relish, after spending several days of forced fasting. When the Mameluke served him a glass of wine, he drank that and, as he swallowed, Napoleon said to him smiling:

– 'Boy, it is a pleasure to drink heartily, I hope that you have assuaged your hunger and thirst.'

– 'I am full, Sire, but I will drink to the health of Your Majesty once again.'

The meal passed in total cordiality and the Emperor plied the *Vélite* with a multitude of questions. On finishing, Desherbiers saluted and returned to his position in the escort.

▲
Chasseurs of the Guard escorting Napoleon. (Illustration by Job, Vinkhuijzen Collection of Military Uniforms, NYPL).

UNIFORMS AND EQUIPMENT

Colback

The typical appearance of a *Guide de Bonaparte*, in Italy and Egypt, is of a soldier sporting a bicorne adorned with *aurore* (orange color) chevrons. This headgear also formed part of the uniform of the *Chasseurs de la Garde*, both Consular and Imperial, but was only used with the *tenue de ville* or *tenue de societé*. For other uniforms, the bicorn was replaced by a colback or busby. The type of colback issued to the *Chasseurs* of the Consular Guard was different from the later, better known model used by the *Chasseurs à cheval de la Garde Impériale* or the elite companies of Hussars and line *Chasseurs*. The version for the consular period was cylindrical in form and not as high as the model for the imperial period. It was covered with short black fur and fitted with a leather chinstrap covered with metal scales. It did not carry the characteristic scarlet *flamme* or bag, but was simply adorned with an *aurore* cord and a short plume of green with a red tip, located on the left side.

It has been repeatedly maintained that the French first discovered the colback in Egypt, where was used by their Turkish enemies, but it is certain that this headgear was already known in France long before. The Hussars of Louis XVI – according to a 1786 water color by Hoffmann –already used it and the Hussars of Frederick the Great wore it as early as 1757. The problem when establishing the date of the adoption of the colback by the Guard *Chasseurs* arises when examining Lejeune's magnificent picture of the Battle of Mount Tabor. In this, a group of *Guides à cheval* are depicted wearing the *colback* during a campaign in which they would have been expected to have worn bicornes. The explanation would appear to be simple: Lejeune painted the picture in 1828 or 1829, and he dressed the *Guides* as he remembered the *Chasseurs* of the imperial period, not as they would have been uniformed during the Egyptian campaign. What is known with total certainty is that the *Chasseurs à cheval* wore the *colback* during the great review carried out by the First Consul in Carrousel Square after *18e Brumaire* as both Carle Vernet and Isabey depict them doing so in contemporary engravings.

In 1801, a new version of the colback appeared. It was virtually the same as the previous one in form and size, except that it had a peak that, like the rest of the hat, was covered with short black fur. The simple cord was replaced by one of braided wool, also in *aurore*, that finished in two

A Captain of *Chasseurs* of the Consular Guard in full dress uniform, Winter 1800-1802. He wears a *colback* with peak, used between 1800 and 1802, which was characterized by having the plume at the front. The pelisses' brown fur edging was used by officers during the Consular period, but not under the Empire. The red trousers are typical of the Consular period with the full dress uniform. He leans on a *l'allemande* sabre. (Illustration by D. A. C.).

▲ Different models of *colback* used by the *Chasseurs* of the Guard. From top to bottom: 1) the first model of the Consular period, 2) the second model of the Consular period, 3), the Empire period model. (Illustration by D. A. C.).

raquettes (flounders) of the same color. This second model colback of the consular period had a scarlet *flamme*, with four *aurore*-piped seams that joined to form a tassel of the same color. The r*aquettes* hung on the left side with the *flamme* on the right. On the front – instead of the left side as in the first model – a larger plume than previously was fitted.

It was probably in 1803 when the classic colback –the one worn by the *Chasseurs à cheval de la Garde Impériale*– entered into service. This consisted of a rigid cylindrical leather frame covered with black bearskin. It measured 250 mm high at the front and 277 mm at the rear. The maximum diameter was 250 mm. The scarlet *flamme* was piped on all four seams with *aurore* cord that joined to form a tassel of the same color, as in the previous model. The *flamme* was fastened at the top of the colback by means of small hooks, and could be removed. On the left side of the colback there was a leather holder into which a large green plume with a red tip and the tricolor insignia was fitted. A braided *aurore* wool cord was formed into two *raquettes*, each one ending in a tassel. The two *raquettes* were united in the upper part by another tassel fitted with a fastener for the plume and insignia attachment thus preventing the *raquettes* from moving about and causing annoyance. The colback was fastened at the top by means of two leather jaws, covered with metal rings. The leather cords that hung from the jaws held the hat in place. If desired, the jaws could be swivelled rearwards, and held by means of a leather fastener that was fastened to a small metal button. During inclement weather, the *flamme* was removed and the colback protected by a black waxed linen cover that attached to the base. The plume was always green tipped scarlet, except for a short period in 1808, when Lefèbvre-Desnoëttes tried to change it for an entirely scarlet one. The concentric circles of the tricolor insignia, from the centre out, were blue, red then white. In 1805 an embroidered yellow eagle was added to the blue centre.

Bicorne

The bicorne was made of black felt. During the consular period, it was low and with the arch little pronounced. Nevertheless, during the imperial period, its height was increased and the arch was made much more pronounced. The consular model had both wings of the same height but, gradually, with the passage of time, the rear wing – the one without the insignia – became considerably higher. It was hemmed with black leather and had an *aurore* chevron holding the insignia. On each wing were lengths of *aurore* cord, "*passants*", and, at each of the two ends, was a pompon, or "chestnut", with a green centre surrounded by *aurore*. Adjacent to the insignia was fixed a green plume tipped scarlet.

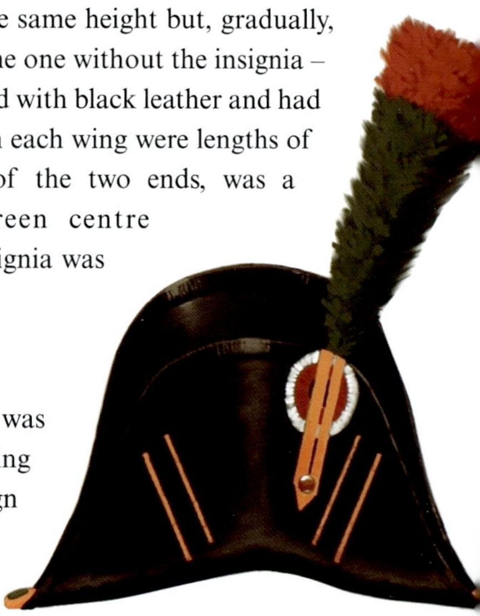

Bonnet de police

The garrison cap or *bonnet de police,* was typical headgear for barracks work, including caring for the horses. It was of a design known as "*à la dragonne*", and remained unaltered during the fifteen years that the *Chasseurs* de la Garde existed. It comprised a cap with an extended sleeve finishing in a point. It was made of green cloth piped *aurore* and, sometimes, edged with scarlet thread. The four seams of the cap's sleeve were decorated with *aurore* cord and, at the tip was sewn a tassel of the same color. An *aurore* hunting horn was attached to the front of the cap - the symbol of the *Chasseurs*.

The uniform "*à la chasseur*" - the dress coat or "*habit*"

The original uniform of the Guard *Chasseurs* was the *habit* type of dress coat with long tails, used by the *Chasseurs* of the Line and *Guides de Bonaparte*. The dress coat known as "*à la chasseur*" remained in use throughout the whole period of the *Chasseurs*' existence. However, its design was modified slightly for some occasions while on some specific campaigns, was replaced with a pelisse or dolman. The dress coat was made from dark green cloth with the collar and pointed cuffs in scarlet. The lapels were formed into three points at the top and, like the tails, were edged with scarlet. Like the lapels, the tails were of the same green cloth as the dress coat. The loops holding the shoulder straps were *aurore*. The hunting horns embroidered on each of the four tail panels were also *aurore* on a scarlet background. The tail of the dress coat had two vertical pockets, "*à soubisse*", edged with scarlet.

Habit veste, the dress coat of the '*à la chasseur*' uniform. Detail of the trefoil shoulder knot. (Illustration by D. A. C.).

The coat had eighteen large, brass buttons, six on each side and one on the upper part of each of the lapels, in the centre of the three cut points (known as "*ecusson*"). The remaining four were distributed in two pairs on the tail pockets. In addition, there were six smaller buttons: two on each cuff and one on each shoulder. On the left shoulder, the dress coat was decorated with an *aurore* wool cord aiguillette that finished in two metallic ferrules that hung on the chest. On the right shoulder, there was trefoil strap made of *aurore* wool. During the consular period and the initial years of the imperial period, each dress coat apron folded back on itself, the fabric of the corners being sewn together at the points. In 1808, the dress coat tails were made much narrower with the tails forming two extended fabric triangles, sewn in such a way as to give the appearance of a false fold. Both triangles were joined by one of their vertices, with a green fabric triangle underneath. This disappeared on the dress coats made at the end of 1810 and the start of 1811.

The uniform "*à la hussarde*"- the dolman and the pelisse

At the end of 1800, the *Chasseurs* of the Guard received the hussar-style uniform with dolman, pelisse and *sabretache* – that would, as full dress, replace the "*à la chasseur*" dress coat for parades and for the *grande tenue* uniform. It would also be used on campaign from 1805, with the exception of the 1806-1807 Polish campaign, where the dress coat "*à la chasseur*" was used.

The dolman was a short jacket made of dark green fabric with the collar in the same color and pointed scarlet cuffs. The front and bottom edges, collar,

▲
Other ranks dolman. (Illustration by D. A. C.).

false pockets and rear seams were edged with a flat *aurore* lace. On the cuffs, a thin braid, a "*soutache*", was sewn in the shape of a trefoil. The *aurore* tape that decorated the rear seams was also bordered with "*soutaches*" culminating in elaborate Hungarian knots. During the Consulate and the first years of the Empire they also used "*soutaches*" in the form of trefoils and loops along the tape that edged the neck and false pockets.

Initially the dolman and pelisse had three rows of 18 buttons down the front. The centre row used large half-round brass ones, with the two outer rows used smaller half-round buttons. Early in 1803, after the new squadrons were formed, the dolmans and pelisses were produced with five rows of buttons. The centre row had large buttons with the four outer rows using smaller ones. The dolman was decorated across the front with double rows of *aurore* braid, which passed horizontally from button to button, with the button placed between the two rows of braid. On the left side, the braid was formed into loops that fastened over the large buttons on the edge of the right side. The rows of braid joined together, forming loops, and ended at the top and bottom rows in trefoils.

A woolen waist sash was worn with the dolman and this consisted of a double skein of dark green wool passing through nine movable scarlet barrels or "*voulants*". The ends of the sash were formed into loops by two scarlet braid bands. On one side, the loops held a length of scarlet wool cord, ending in green tassels whilst, on the other side, was a scarlet toggle. The longer cord, which was doubled, had a series of green knots along part of its length to form positions to retain the toggle. Initially, the color of the end tassels could have been either green or red. This lack of uniformity caused Eugène de Beauharnais to order, in April 1803, that a green tassel must be used by all *Chasseurs*.

The pelisse was made of scarlet cloth and it is possible that the first ones issued were lined with white sheepskin. Later, the lining was white flannel. The pelisse was edged with short black sheepskin. It was decorated in much the same way as the dolman, with gold-yellow braid, lace and *soutaches*. There were sixteen large buttons on the pelisse; eighteen down the front on the right side, and a further eight (occasionally only six), at the bottom of the rear seam laces. The remaining rows had smaller buttons. It was also fitted with a cord and toggle to support the pelisse when slung over the left shoulder. Both the cord and the toggle were made from *aurore* wool. The Chasseurs, with the exception of the officers, had no flounders at the end of the suspension cords. When the pelisse was worn as a jacket it was fastened by the top four buttons only and, because of this, the top four braid loops on the left side of the pelisse were longer than the others. These loops had to pass

Other ranks pelisse. (Illustration by D. A. C.). ▶

over two thickness of sheepskin edging. The bottom of the pelisse would thus be somewhat open towards the bottom, and the waistcoat could be seen at this point. (It should be noted that the dolman was not worn beneath the pelisse.) The cuffs of the pelisse were also edged with black sheepskin and the cuff braid formed a spearhead shape, inside which was a strip of black sheepskin.

Waistcoat

The waistcoat was worn beneath the coat, the dolman or the pelisse. It had two basic designs, one decorated with *aurore* braid and the other plain. The braided waistcoat was made from scarlet cloth, sometimes with, sometimes without a stand-up collar, and was edged with flat *aurore* lace and ornamented with similar color *soutaches*, forming horizontal rows and incorporating buttonholes. Initially, the waistcoat had three rows of fifteen buttons, increasing to sixteen in 1807, and finally, in 1812, to eighteen. The plain waistcoat was also scarlet with, initially, cross-over lapels and two rows of fifteen buttons but, by 1807, it appears to have been changed to a simpler design, buttoning down the centre with a single row of buttons. The plain waistcoat does not appear to have been manufactured after 1809, since it does not show on the tailors' invoices.

A green cloth stable waistcoat was used for fatigue duties worn with the linen trousers described below. This waistcoat was double-breasted, with two rows of ten brass buttons and one brass button on each cuff. The garment had a stand-up collar almost as high as that of the coat.

Officer of *Chasseurs* of the Consular Guard in '*à la chasseur*' uniform, 1800-1802. He is shown at the time when officers began to use the characteristic red leather belts as worn by this officer. The bandolier he wears is also of red leather – although they could also be green leather –edged with decorative gold motifs. The *schabraque* is trimmed with gold and edged with a red fabric lace. The *schabraque* tassel is typical of the time although, later, it was discarded as it got in the way when tying back the *schabraque*. (Illustration by D. A. C.).

Trousers

Over a period of time, several forms of breeches were worn for full dress. One of these remained in use as part of the service dress and one disappeared entirely. While still wearing the basic dress of the *Guides*, the *Chasseurs* wore green Hungarian-style breeches with *aurore* lace on the side seams forming Hungarian knots at the openings of the front flap. The seam laces followed the usual hussar pattern in that they joined each other on the seat of the breeches forming, at their juncture, a loop,

In November 1800, with the introduction of hussar style dress, these breeches were replaced for parade wear and full dress by breeches of scarlet cloth bearing the same *aurore* lace decoration. The green breeches were limited for use with the '*petite tenue*' or service dress with the coat.

▲

Chasseurs of the Imperial Guard wearing cloaks. These *Chasseurs* wear the cloak with cape and sleeves that entered service in 1812. (Watercolor by L. Rousselot, Anne S. K. Brown Collection)

Probably in late 1802 or early 1803, creamy yellow buckskin breeches were introduced with scarlet breeches being discontinued. The buckskin breeches were similar in cut to the hussar style, closing with a flap at the front and narrowing towards the ankles. On the march and on campaign, the *Chasseurs*, as with most units, tended to wear something more robust. This was usually a form of trouser which was cut to fit more loosely and, generally, had the inside leg reinforced with either leather or a double thickness of cloth. During the Consular period, the *Chasseurs* wore *pantalons de cheval* of green cloth, reinforced with skin and opening down the sides. Down the outer closing edges were stripes of red cloth fitted with buttonholes. The *pantalons* were secured with eighteen brass buttons down each side. In 1808, they were replaced with trousers of green cloth that were reinforced with buckskin and had an *aurore* lace stripe covering the outer seams. Yet another change occurred in 1811, when a new style of *pantalons de cheval* was introduced. These were again of green cloth but lacked any visible reinforcing, though probably the inside leg and the seat was made from two layers of cloth. On the side seams were double stripes of *aurore* lace. This was the style mainly worn during the Russian campaign and for the greater part of the 1813 campaign. At the end of 1813, the color of the *pantalons* was changed to steel grey. These were also in the form of trousers and were reinforced with either skin or cloth, and had a double red stripe down each outer seam. During the first restoration, the style changed yet again and reverted to the original design of green cloth, reinforced with buckskin and with a red stripe fitted with eighteen brass buttons.

Fatigue trousers, used with the stable jacket, were made from unbleached linen or coarse cloth and opened down the outer seams. They were fastened on each side by eighteen bone buttons.

▶

Chasseurs of the Guard in *tenue d'ecurie* and *tenue de ville* uniforms. The fatigue dress used for working in the stables had a number of variations. This illustration shows a *chasseur* wearing leggings, these were only used for this purpose - never with any other type of uniform. The other *chasseur* wears the *tenue de ville* uniform, the prescribed uniform for Sundays in summer, with the dolman fastened with both upper buttons only, the decorated red waistcoat, green Hungarian trousers, sabre and *sabretache*. Note the rear decoration on the dolman. (Illustration by D. A. C.).

Cloaks

For the greater part of their existence, the *Chasseurs* used a cloak that basically remained unchanged. It was made of green cloth, without sleeves, had a stand up collar and was equipped with a short cape. At first these capes were very short, just covering the shoulders and were removable. In February 1804, longer capes, reaching the waist, were delivered to the *Chasseurs.* An Order of the Day states that: "these capes serve firstly to be worn over the cloak when "*en route*", secondly for service on foot, thirdly for protection in bad weather when on escort duty to the First Consul, during which service the cloak is not worn'. It is probable that the short capes were withdrawn at this time. The issue of the separate cape does not appear to have lasted long as no mention appears on the stores lists for 1804 and 1805. Assuming that there was only the original issue, it could be presumed that after around 1807, there were no more separate cloaks, except possibly for the escort troop.

In 1812, there is mention of a cloak-coat. This is one equipped with sleeves. We assume that from this date either type could be worn as both types appear on the clothing lists.

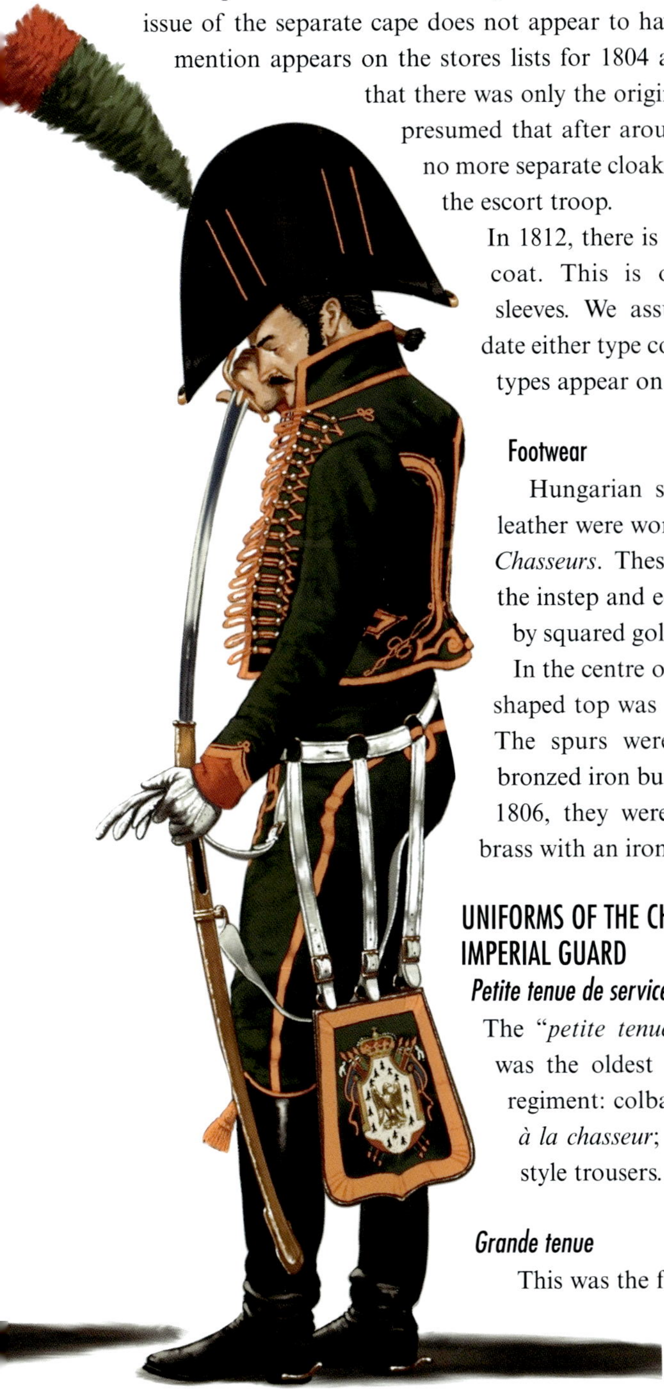

▲ Sergeant major in *redingote* and groom. The redingote was a work frock coat used by Chasseur officers and sergeant majors when in barracks. Before ten in the morning, the redingote was worn with the garrison cap, but after that it had to be worn with a bicorne. (Illustration by M. Benigni. The Author's collection).

Footwear

Hungarian style boots of black leather were worn at all times by the *Chasseurs*. These were pleated over the instep and edged around the top by squared gold-yellow wool braid. In the centre of the V of the heart-shaped top was a gold-yellow tassel. The spurs were initially made of bronzed iron but, towards the end of 1806, they were probably made of brass with an iron rowel.

UNIFORMS OF THE CHASSEURS OF THE IMPERIAL GUARD

Petite tenue de service

The "*petite tenue*" or basic uniform was the oldest and simplest in the regiment: colback, green dress coat *à la chasseur*; vest and Hungarian style trousers.

Grande tenue

This was the full dress uniform. In winter, the use of the pelisse, worn over the vest was obligatory, whereas in summer the vest, dolman and the sash were worn together with the pelisse, hanging from the left shoulder. In 1801, in summer as in winter, red trousers were worn and, from the end of 1802, buckskin trousers. The *colback* was worn, with the plume and *sabretache* without protective covers, so that they shone in all their glory. The snaffle rein of the horse's harness was *aurore*, instead of the normal one of black leather.

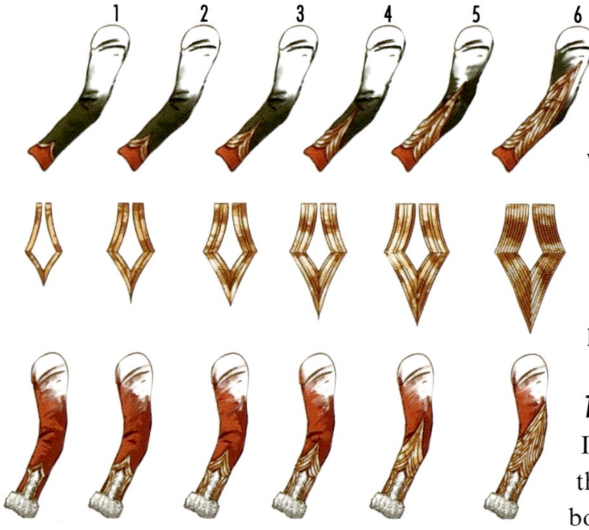

▲ OFFICERS: on the dolman, the Hungarian trousers and the pelisse. 1 Second Lieutenant; 2 First Lieutenant; 3 Captain; 4 *Chef d'escadron;* 5 Colonel in second; 6 *Colonel Major.*

Tenue d'escorte

In the uniform for mounted escort duties or picket functions the fastened pelisse or dolman with the sash was worn. In both cases, they wore buckskin trousers and covered *sabretaches*. Nevertheless, between 18.00 and 06.00 hours they could wear the green fabric riding breeches. For the same service on foot, an identical uniform was worn but the *sabretache* was used without a cover. A covered *colback* could be used in bad weather and on horseback. These regulations were applicable on campaign, except that of 1806-1807, when they used the dress coat "*à la chasseur*", vest and trousers of green fabric, but without a *sabretache* which was only used with the uniform "*à la hussarde*".

In order to distinguish the Chasseurs on escort duty to the Emperor, these wore the short cape. The troops not on escort duty wore the cloak.

▶ *Chasseurs* of the Guard during the Polish campaign of 1807. The *Chasseur* on the left is in foot escort uniform, which meant he had to carry a fixed bayonet. The mounted *Chasseur* is foraging, as one can see from the straw carried on the back of his horse. On the right the *Chasseur* carries a hanging pouch with feed for the horse. The carbine is on the left side, something not prescribed but, nevertheless, very common. Given what he is doing, it is unnecessary to have the plume fitted to the *colback*, for that reason only the insignia is visible. (Illustration by D. A. C.).

Tenue de campagne

On each campaign, the uniform of the *Chasseurs* of the Guard varied, although the predominant one was the hussar style, with the pelisse or dolman. For anyone on the following campaigns, the cape was always available in case of bad weather.

Campaign of Austerlitz (1805): pelisse.
Campaign of Poland (1807): dress coat "*à la chasseur*".
Campaign of Spain (1808): pelisse.
Campaigns between 1809 and 1815: dolman and sash, without pelisse - neither fastened nor hung on the shoulder.

NCOs and other ranks: on the dolman and the pelisse. 1, *brigadier;* 2, *maréchal des logis;* 3, *maréchal des logis chef.* ▼

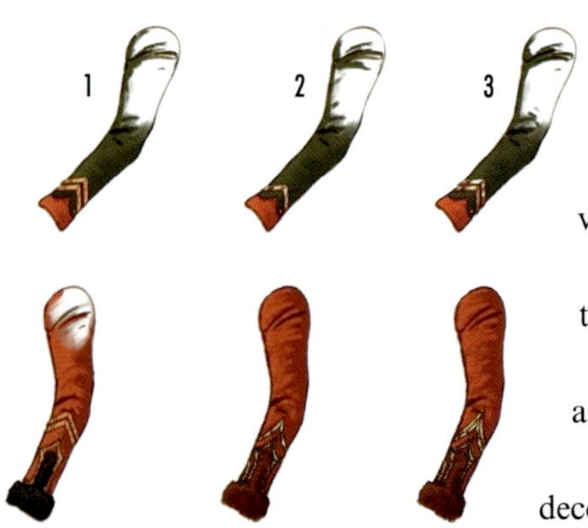

Tenue de ville

The walking-out uniform had different variants depending on the day of the week and the time of the year, although at all times, they wore the bicorne with plume and the boots "*à la Souvarov*".

Winter (October to April): dress coat "*à la chasseur*", decorated red vest, green Hungarian trousers, sabre without *sabretache*.

Sundays in winter: pelisse, decorated red vest, green Hungarian trousers and sabre without *sabretache*.

Summer (May to September): dress coat "*à la chasseur*" with vest and trousers of white cotton. Sabre without *sabretache*.

Sundays in summer: Dolman only fastened by both upper buttons, decorated red vest, green Hungarian trousers and sabre with *sabretache*.

▲
Sabre "à la Marengo" of a senior Chasseurs officer of the Imperial Guard. This ornate weapon was not used in combat, only in parades. The blade was profusely decorated and shows a crowned eagle next to the inscription "Chasseurs à cheval de la Garde Impériale". The scabbard was gilded bronze and was decorated with an eagle and other designs like those seen in the image.

▶
Captain of Chasseurs of the Imperial Guard in parade uniform in 1805. The pelisse is edged with Arctic fox fur and he wears doeskin trousers. His *sabretache* is edged with gold ribbon and his sabre is '*à la Marengo*'. Finally, the *schabraque* is leopard skin edged with gold and piped red with green outer edging. All these elements combine to clearly indicate that he is an officer aside, of course, from the captain's chevrons displayed on the dolman and pelisse. (Illustration by D. A. C.).

Tenue d'écurie

The uniform for work in the stables was very simple: garrison cap, green short jacket with a line of nine or twelve buttons and trousers of white linen with a line of eighteen buttons on each leg.

Variations in the uniforms and equipment of the officers of the Chasseurs à cheval of the Imperial Guard

Colback: the only difference with respect to the troops was that the *raquettes*, as well as the decorative elements of the *flamme* (cord on seams and tassel) were gilt, rather than aurore.

Bicorne: cord and *passants* in gilt instead of aurore. It had gold tassels and not pompons – at each end.

Garrison cap: identical to the troopers' cap, except that the decorative elements were gold instead of *aurore*.

Pelisse: the fur was sewn to the collar, edges and cuffs were white fox. The connecting cord and accompanying *raquettes,* hanging on the right side of the chest, were gold. All the decorative elements were in gilt, including the buttons.

Dolman: all the decorative elements (clasps, *soutaches*, borders) were in gold. The sash was green, but the cylinders through which the cord passed were gilt, like the connecting cord of the sash.

Dress coat: of the same color and cut as that of the troops, but made of better quality cloth. On the right shoulder was a shoulder knot and, on the left, an epaulette, both of the same color as the hunting horns on the tails.

Trousers: similar to those of the troops but in better quality cloth. They could be red in the *tenue de ville* or white for the *tenue de societé*. The loops in the green Hungarian style trousers were not undecorated, but had embroidery in the form of spear points pointing downwards. The number of loops on the trousers corresponded to the wearer's rank.

Boots: aside from traditional black, they were also occasionally red or green, according to the individual officer's taste.

Belt: in red leather, identical to the sabre and *sabretache* securing straps. It had metal roundels bearing an imperial eagle.

Cartridge holder bandolier: in green leather bordered in gold. Adorned with an eagle and a crown joined by a chain. Sometimes it was protected with a red leather cover.

Sabretache: for full dress uniform it was bordered with gold ribbon, instead of the *aurore* of the troops.

Schabraque: of green cloth, identical to the troopers, but with the chevron in gold. Also a leopard skin one was used for parades and other events;

Leopard skin *schabraque* used by the officers in *grande tenue,* or full dress uniforms.
▼

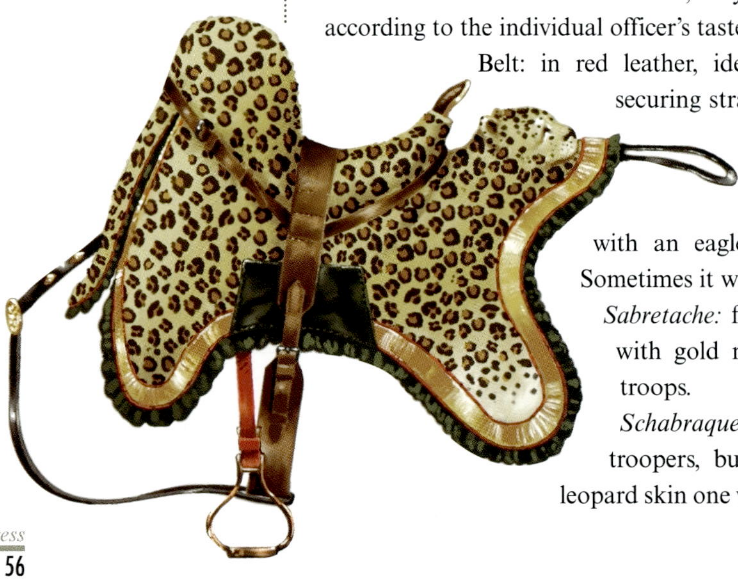

Maréchal des logis in full dress uniform. (Watercolor by L. Rousselot, Anne S. K. Brown Collection)

this was green cloth with leopard skin on the saddle pommel.

Sabre: the one commonly used by the officers was the light cavalry model ANX with three guards. They also carried a "*à la Marengo*" sabre, profusely decorated with a lion head on the hilt. With the *tenue de ville* or *societé*, a dress sword, or epée, was carried instead of a sabre.

Variations in the uniforms and equipment of the trumpeters of the *Chasseurs à cheval* of the Imperial Guard

Trumpeters were outfitted in much the same way as the rest of the *Chasseurs*, but the colors of the plume and clothing were different, and there were many more adornments in the form of borders and *soutaches* in gold. Below is an explanation of some of the more evident differences between the troops and trumpeters of the *Chasseurs á cheval de la Garde Impériale*:

Colback: there were two models. One in white fur for parades and another of black fur for use on campaign, both equipped with a sky blue plume tipped with crimson. The flounders and tassels were crimson and gold.

Bicorne: chevrons and *passants* in gold. At each end was a crimson pompon surrounded by gold.

Garrison cap: identical to that of the troops but in sky blue, piped with gold and with a gold tassel.

Pelisse: crimson with piping and decorative clasps in sky blue and gold.

Dolman: sky blue with crimson piping and gold decorative clasps.

Dress coat: made in sky blue cloth. Adorned on the left shoulder with a crimson and gold braided cord and, on the right with a shoulder knot in the form of a trefoil made of gold wool cord.

Waistcoat: of scarlet cloth, with five rows of buttons; the piping and soutaches were of tape or cord in a mixture of sky blue and gold. On campaign or for marches, they wore a waistcoat without ornament, like the rest of the *Chasseurs*.

Trousers: they had buckskin riding breeches, like the rest of the *Chasseur*s. The Hungarian-style trousers were sky blue with *soutaches* in crimson and gold.

Sabretache: sky blue background piped with gold and with the imperial coat of arms. They also used the plain black leather *sabretache* with a brass crowned eagle.

Schabraque: sky blue piped with gold, edged red with a hunting horn or a crowned eagle at the corners, both in gold.

Trumpet: traditionally of brass, but silver plated with the full dress uniform

THE NON-COMMISSIONED OFFICERS

Chasseurs of the Imperial Guard. *Maréchal des logis* and *Chasseurs*. This sergeant major and his men wear the full dress uniform. The sergeant major differentiated from the enlisted men by the eagle on the *schabraque* being embroidered in gold thread, his pelisse being trimmed in marmot fur and the soutache braids on the dolman and pelisse in green and gold. All the above was in addition to the chevrons indicating the wearer's rank. In this case, the single inverted 'V' chevron on the forearm indicates that he is a *maréchal des logis* while the chevron on the upper arm indicates ten years service and, therefore, that he has gained an extra franc per day. Two galloons on the arm indicated fifteen years service, and a franc and a half per day extra; three galloons on the arm twenty years service and two francs extra per day.

On the '*à la chasseur*' uniform the difference between troopers and sergeant-majors was primarily noticeable because the braid of the aiguillette, shoulder knots and *soutaches* on the trousers being in scarlet wool and gold, and not *aurore*, the usual color of these elements of the uniform for the other ranks.

Chasseurs à cheval of the Imperial Guard: *trompette* in full dress uniform and *vélite*. (Illustration by D. A. C.).

Chasseur of the Young Guard in 1813. The most characteristic feature of the *Chasseurs* of the Young Guard was the red shako. This was prevented from being lost in, say, a charge by the cords attached to the rear. The *Chasseur* leans on his Model ANX light cavalry sabre, characterised by its three-bar guard. The figure shows how the carbine was attached to the bandolier. (Illustration by D. A. C.).

with cords in crimson and gold. At the beginning of the Imperial period, it was decorated with a green guidon-shaped fabric banner with leaves, a hunting horn and the letters EF (Empire Français). Later, the banner became square with a crimson background decorated with the imperial coat of arms.

Arms: they were equipped with the same model sabre as the troops and an ANIX Model cavalry pistol. They were not issued with a carbine or bayonet.

Uniform and equipment of the vélites

The *vélites* were the sons of rich families who paid for the privilege to go on Imperial Duty as cadets. During their existence, from September 1805 to August 1811, the *vélites* of the *Chasseurs à cheval de la Garde Impériale* were uniformed "*à la chasseur*", that is to say with dress coat, waistcoat with or without ornament, green riding breeches and a bicorne with plume. The arms and equipment were identical to those of its elder brethren. The horse harnesses were also identical to the *Chasseu*rs, except for the lambswool *schabraque* which was edged in red - reminiscent of the *Chasseurs* of the Consular Guard - and which was used exclusively by the *vélites* during the Imperial period.

Uniform and equipment of the Chasseurs of the Young Guard

The squadrons of the *Chasseurs* of the Young Guard were identical to those of the Old Guard - dolman, sash, waistcoat, green riding breeches, cape and garrison cap. The only difference was that the fabric used for the preparation of these articles was of inferior quality. There are some doubts about other elements of the uniform and equipment, due to the short existence of this formation. For example, there is some controversy as to whether the *Chasseurs* of the Young Guard used the scarlet pelisse or not. There are at least two possibilities: it is possible that the use of the pelisse was contained in the regulations - as some authors affirm - but that these regulations were never implemented; or it could be that some *Chasseurs* of the Young Guard took pelisses issued to them during the time that they served with the Old Guard.

The greatest difference in the uniform of the *Chasseurs* of the Young Guard was the use, by troops and sergeant majors, of the "*shako rouleau*": a tall, red, cylindrical shako, with gold insignia, a gold-yellow, red or green pompon and a green plume with a scarlet tip.

The bandoleers were white but, unlike the squadrons of the Old Guard, were without seams. The *sabretache* was black leather with a metal eagle or the coat of arms of the Empire.

The *schabraque* color was different to that of the *Chasseurs* of the Old Guard. Rousselot affirms that it was scarlet piped green; a lambswool covered the pommel and it had no corner decoration. The valise was also scarlet with a green border.

In spite of what has been written, it is necessary to take into account that many corporals and sergeant majors came from the squadrons of the Old Guard and that, therefore, many of them would have retained their old uniform during the final years of the Empire when re-supply was difficult.

It appears that the officers had all decorations in gold and that these were certainly shown on pelisses, but with black fur edging, not white as those of officers of the *Chasseurs* of the Old Guard.

The timbalier Bruno Lemoine in full dress uniform. (Watercolor by L. Rousselot, Anne S. K. Brown Collection)

The *timbalier* Bruno Lemoine

When Napoleon formed the Consular Guard in 1800, he also reinstated the rank of *timbalier* (kettle drummer) in the French army, which had been suppressed in 1776. Among the regiments that had *timbaliers* were the *Chasseurs* of the Guard. There is little existing information on the *timbalier* uniform. However, two types of uniforms used by them are known and of which there are quite reasonable reconstructions: the Mameluke style and the hussar style with white colback, also used by trumpeters. It is conceivable that the first type of single uniform was used only for parades, whereas the second would have been used on campaign.

The kettledrum was never used by the *timbalier* on campaign, only for parades – they were fitted with aprons of the same green-piped-gold fabric as the *schabraque*. In the Musée de l'Armée in Paris, is preserved the central part of the *sabretache*, decorated with musical instruments on a scarlet background, that belonged to *timbalier*, Bruno Lemoine.

With the uniform in hussar-style, the pelisse of a *timbalier* was scarlet, as the rest of the troop. The drum aprons and *schabraque* were scarlet and decorated with a double gold stripe.

The most famous of the regiment's *timbaliers* was, without doubt, Bruno Lemoine, who reached the rank of *brigadier-trompette* and who was killed in Spain, during the combat of Torquemada in 1808.

EQUIPMENT

The equipment initially issued to the *Chasseurs* in 1800 comprised the following: a pouch, without decoration, a pouch belt, a carbine belt, a waist belt and white gloves with cuffs. With the change to hussar-style dress, the

▲
Different models of *sabretache*. Left to right: Republican period, service *sabretache* of the Empire period, other ranks *sabretache* of *Chasseurs* of the Imperial Guard. (Illustration by D. A. C.).

form of the waist belt was altered to accommodate the *sabretache*. The pouch was made of black leather with, it would appear, the flap having a straight edge, later changing to a flap cut "*en accolade*". The pouch was carried on a white-buff leather belt with brass fittings. The carbine belt was also of white-buff leather with brass fittings and a steel swivel clip, into which the ring on the slide of the carbine was fixed. Also, on this steel fitting, was a small white leather strap with a brass buckle. This strap was passed around the small of the carbine butt to hold it steady. The waist belt was of white buff leather and fastened by means of an "S" hook, with an adjusting buckle, and made from three lengths of leather. The three lengths were joined together by two brass rings, through which the sabre carrying straps passed. With the change to hussar-style dress in November 1800, certain changes were introduced with regard to the *Chasseurs*' equipment: the belts were now stitched along the borders, as was the practice with the rest of the Consular troops and, later, those of the Imperial Guard, and the brass fittings were more elaborate. With the adoption of the *sabretache*, a change in the design of the waist belt was again necessary. From this time, the belt consisted of four sections joined by three brass rings to accommodate the three straps of the *sabretache*. The waist belt was 34 mm wide. One section was 890 mm long and fitted with an adjusting buckle and a slide. This piece had a fitting, which the belt passed through and to which the "S" hook was attached. The two middle sections were 81 mm long and the fourth 203 mm long. The latter had a fitting into which the end of the "S" hook fastened.

▲
Detail of *Chasseurs*' equipment. (Watercolor by François Gerard).

In September 1803, with the introduction of new arms for the *Chasseur*, a white leather bayonet frog was introduced. This item was removable and fastened to that section of the waist belt between the shortest strap of the sabre and the centre strap of the *sabretache*, by a brass button which passed through a slit in the waist belt.

For the entire period of the Empire, the following description applies to the equipment in use: The pouch of black leather remained the same with the flap "*en accolade*" and without decoration until 1809, when a new pouch was introduced which was a little smaller overall and with the flap embossed with a brass crowned eagle. The pouch belt remained the same, with the edges stitched, the metal fittings consisting of a buckle, a slide, a strengthening plate at the end of the belt and a button of yellow copper at each end of the belt. These buttons served to fasten the belt through the carrying rings of the pouch. The pouch-belt was 50 mm wide and approximately 1m 461 mm long and consisted of two parts. One was 1m 71 mm long and the other 390 mm long. The longest ended in the brass plate and the shorter piece ended in the buckle with the slide.

The carbine belt was also stitched along the edges and was slightly wider than the pouch belt, with the same metal fittings except for two metal buttons. The carbine belt was 81 mm wide and was 1m 705 mm long. The carbine belt had a double headed "button", which passed through a slit in the carbine belt and through a slit in the pouch belt, thus joining the two together on the chest. Also fitted to the carbine belt was a steel slide with a swivel clip, into which the ring on the slide of the carbine fixed. A white leather strap was attached to this fitting, and could be passed around the small of the butt of the carbine, to hold it firmly in place. The only additional point to make regarding this piece of equipment is that the rings were stitched to the belt sections in such a way as to allow movement of the sections around the rings.

▲ Chasseur with his horse and full equipment during the 1812 campaign. (Illustration by M. Benigni. The Author's collection).

With the introduction of new carbines with bayonets, a white leather lock cover was provided. This was shaped to fit over the lock mechanism and trigger guard, the pieces being stitched together and the opening fastened by two small straps and brass buckles.

The most important innovation with the adoption of the hussar dress was the *sabretache*, the "trademark" of the light cavalry that, for the *Chasseurs*, became one of the most ornate in the whole French army.

During the Consular period, the *sabretache's* face was covered with red cloth and decorated with emblems of the Republic. At the top was a white cloth scroll bearing the inscription, in black thread, "*Garde des Consuls*". Centrally, beneath the scroll, was a small circlet of green laurel leaves. Beneath this was a large white hunting horn. Superimposed on the horn was the "Lictor's Fasces" in blue, bound with white straps. Passing through the fasces, was a white halberd, below which was a large white bow. This bow was at the junction of two branches that encircled the design. Embroidered in two shades of green, the branches were palm leaves on the left side and oak leaves on the right. Several variations existed for the layout of the decoration and the color of the fasces. Around the edge was a strip of *aurore* wool lace, woven in a bar pattern. This lace was edged on its inner side with an *aurore soutache*. The *sabretache* itself was made of brown leather, which appeared as an edging on the outside of the *aurore* lace.

With the formation of the Empire, the design of the *sabretache* changed both in decoration and, it would appear, in shape as well. The new shape was somewhat squatter than that used during the Consular period.

Model 1803 sabre of the *Chasseurs* of the Imperial Guard. (Illustration by D. A. C.).

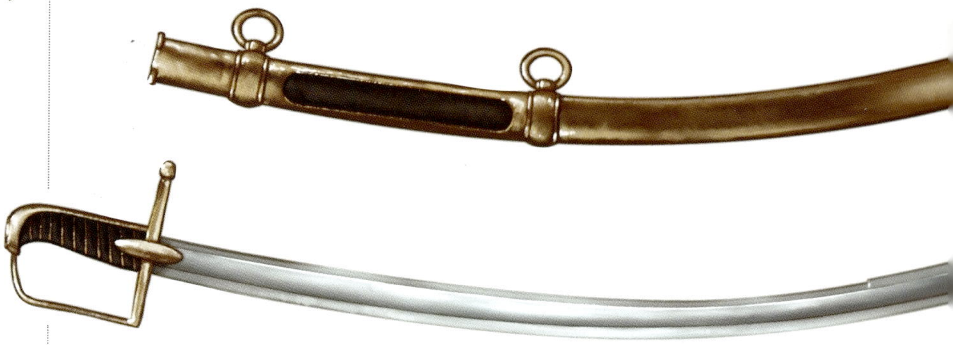

Sabre *à l'allemande* used by officers of the *Chasseurs* of the Consular Guard. (Illustration by D. A. C.).

TECHNICAL DETAILS OF THE SABRE ISSUED TO THE *CHASSEURS À CHEVAL DE LA GARDE*

Length of blade: 855 to 860 mm
Curvature of the blade: 65 to 72 mm
Length of the upper part of the scabbard: 65 to 74 mm
Diameter of the scabbard hoops: 22 to 24 mm.
Curvature of the scabbard: 62 to 74 mm
Inner diameter of the scabbard: 23 mm
Outer diameter of the scabbard: 25 mm
Space between the hoops: 215 to 250 mm
Length of the sword knot: 170 to 180 mm
Length of the Boutrolle (commonly called the drag)
Before 1810: 95 mm
From 1811-1812: 115 mm
From 1812-1813: 150 mm
Weight of the blade: 0.65 kg

Basically, the *sabretache* used during the Empire period had a green cloth background edged with *aurore* wool lace, woven in a wavy pattern. In the centre was the Imperial mantle surmounted by a crown. On the mantle was an eagle, while behind the mantle were light green, crimson and sky blue *guidons*.

The early models had the Imperial crown, the mantle, the eagle and the *guidons* cut from cloth and sewn to the face of the green cloth. *Aurore* cloth covered the edges of these items. The pikes, cravats, fringes, staffs and the butts of the pikes were embroidered in colored wools. The crown was basically yellow, with a crimson interior. The crown trefoil leaf designs were light green edged with gold-yellow cord. The base of the crown, which was also yellow edged gold-yellow, contained a number of ovals, representing jewels, surrounded by silver "pearls".

The central oval was crimson, flanked by light green ovals, while the two half-ovals at the edges, were again crimson. The mantle itself was crimson, lined white. Upon the white lining appeared black ermine markings. The edges of the mantle were bordered by *aurore* lace that, in turn, was edged with *aurore* cords, and decorated with *aurore* stitching. The *guidons* appearing at the top edges of the mantle were, from the crown outwards; light green, crimson and sky-blue. The pike-heads, staffs and fringes were *aurore*, while the cravats at the top of the staffs were white with *aurore* fringes. The ribbon crossing the sky-blue *guidon* was *aurore*. At the bottom of the mantle, the staffs were embroidered to correspond to the color of the *guidons*, and the butts were *aurore*. In the centre of the mantle was an Imperial eagle, embroidered in yellow wool and shaded with brown wools. On the inside of the *aurore* edging lace was a *soutache* of *aurore*. Later it would appear, only the white of the cloak was of cloth. All the remaining ornamentation was embroidered in colored wools, outlined by *aurore* cords, and the embroidered eagle was replaced by a brass stamping. The model in use at the close of the Empire period was identical to that described but the surrounding stripe had lost the *soutache*. The *sabretache* was carried on straps 34 mm wide.

Except for parades and other special occasions, a black-varnished linen sheath or cover known as a "*couvre-sabretache*" protected this elaborate, fragile accessory. This cover was, at first, plain but, by 1812, was decorated with a yellow painted crowned eagle. There also exists the possibility that the *Chasseurs* used a "service" *sabretache* of plain black leather, decorated with a brass crowned eagle, similar to that issued to the Young Guard squadrons.

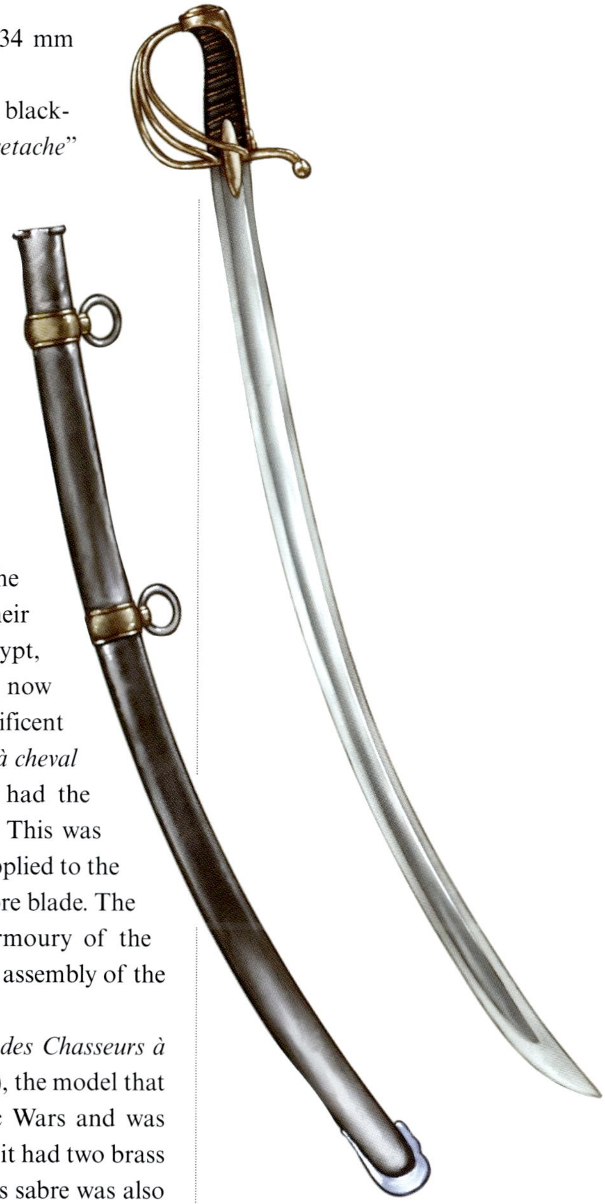

▲ A light cavalry officer's sabre. The model used by *Chasseurs* of the Guard officers had gilt scabbard rings. Note the characteristic three-bar guard. The same model was issued to light cavalry troopers, the only difference being that it had steel suspension rings. (Illustration by D. A. C.).

ARMAMENT

Chasseurs à cheval de la Garde sabre

In 1800, Napoleon felt that a distinguished unit, like the *Chasseurs à cheval* of the Consular, should be equipped with their own model sabre. The *Guides* Model 1786, used in Italy and Egypt, was the "*à l'allemande*" light cavalry sabre, but it was now imperative to equip to the Guard elite horsemen with a magnificent weapon that would be given the title of "*Sabre des Chasseurs à cheval de la Garde des Consuls 1e modèle 1800-1803*". This sabre had the inscription "*Manufre de Klingenthal*" inscribed on the blade. This was the only piece made by the prestigious Alsatian factory and supplied to the French army from the mid XVII century and was the finest sabre blade. The remainder of the troops had sabres manufactured at the armoury of the equally prestigious Nicolas Boutet, located in Versailles, where assembly of the weapons took place.

On 22nd September 1803, the *Chasseurs* received the *Sabre des Chasseurs à cheval de la Garde Consulaire* - later *Impériale* - (*2e modèle 1803*), the model that would be used throughout the remainder of the Napoleonic Wars and was slightly different from the previous one in size and the fact that it had two brass hoops added to the scabbard, with an appliqué of leather. This sabre was also fitted with the Klingenthal blade at Versailles. The inscription on the blade read: "*Mfture Nale de Klingenthal Colaux frères Entreprs*" or "*Mfure Impale du Klingenthal Coulaux frères*", although other variants can also be found, such as the same inscription on the blade of the first model.

In 1810, the Guard *Chasseurs*' sabre underwent small modifications. The scabbard began to be made as a single piece and the grip became a little larger. The revised name for the weapon was *Sabre des Chasseurs à cheval de la Garde Impériale – 3e type*. This is not to say that there were three models of sabre issued during the Napoleonic period as this implied that a new model replaced an earlier one. Many *Chasseurs* preferred one model to another and resisted any change.

In addition, although units of the Guard *Chasseurs* were the first to receive any new model sabre, they were also eventually issued to troopers and sergeant-majors of the Horse Artillery, the *Train d'Artillerie* of the Guard and the Hussars of the Guard of the Kingdom of Holland, later to become

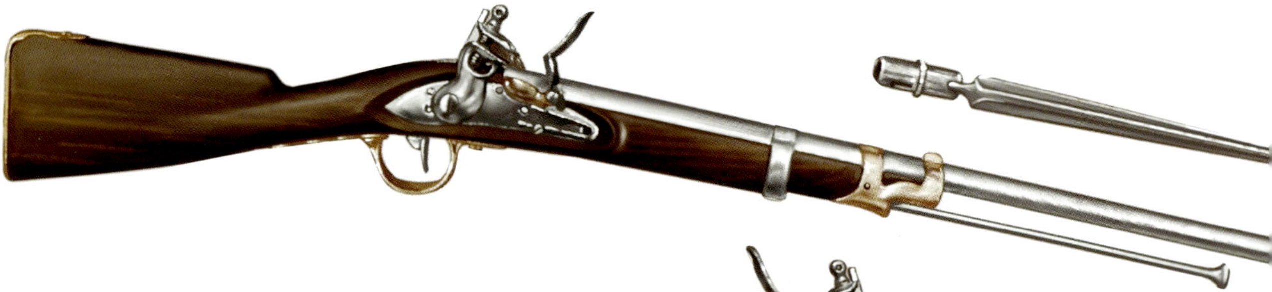

▲ Model 1786 light cavalry carbine. From 1803, this weapon could be fitted with a bayonet. The hoop on the rear served to hold the weapon on a hook on the bandolier. (Illustration by D. A. C.).

known as the famous Red Lancers of the Imperial Guard.

In the beginning, the sword knot was made of white leather ending in a braided tassel of the same color. In 1812, the leather strap was replaced with a woolen cord that was retained at the end with a braided woolen tassel.

The carbine

During the Consular period, the *Chasseurs* were armed with a carbine similar to the Model 1786 used by the Hussars, although it is almost certain that many of them would not have had this weapon and would have been issued with muskets with a shortened barrel or carbines of foreign manufacture. At the end of 1800 the Model 1800 carbine appeared and was quickly put into general use. In September 1803 the *Chasseurs* were issued with a new model carbine. This featured a bayonet practically identical to that used by the infantry. In fact, this carbine was no more than the Model 1786 with the barrel modified to accept the bayonet. It was the same as that issued with the Model AN IX musket and measured 48.7 cm in length. This had a chestnut cowhide scabbard that connected to the middle sword belt by a white leather frog.

Cavalry Pistols. From the end of the Consular period to the close of the Empire, both AN IX and AN XIII models were used. 80,000 of the first model and over 300,000 of the second were manufactured. (Illustration by D. A. C.). ▼

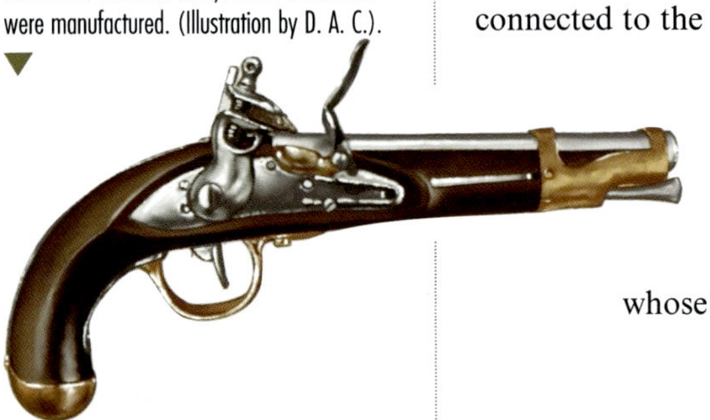

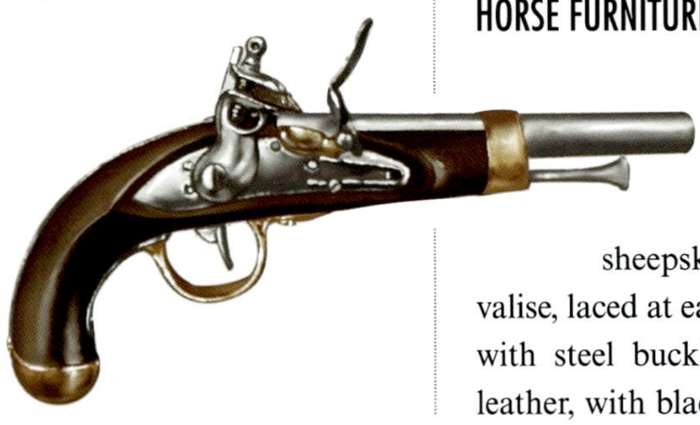

The pistols

At the end of the consular period, the pistols used by the *Chasseurs* were the Model AN IX, used throughout the imperial period together with the popular Model AN XIII, whose issue was more generalized.

HORSE FURNITURE

The Regiment of *Chasseurs à cheval* of the Imperial Guard used to ride chestnut or sorrel horses and only the trumpeters and the timbalier rode dapple ones.

The original horse furniture consisted of a white sheepskin, edged with red dog-toothing, and with a green cylindrical valise, laced at each end by a ring of *aurore* lace. The bridles were black leather with steel buckles and brass ornaments. The stirrup leathers were cream leather, with blackened steel stirrups. The bit was made of steel and curved in the light cavalry fashion. The girth strap was grey and the surcingle was black. In September 1800, a cloth *schabraque* was introduced for parade wear, while sheepskin was retained for service wear. By 1805 sheepskins were used solely by the *vélites*.

The saddle used under the sheepskin was the traditional hussar or Hungarian style, with a saddlebow of wood. A new style saddle for use with the cloth *schabraque* was distributed to NCO's in 1803, and, by 1805, the whole regiment was equipped with them. This saddle was made of leather with panels and flaps. It was sometimes referred to as the saddle "*à la anglaise*". The saddle was fitted with two holsters, straps to hold the valise at the rear, and straps to hold the cloak at the front. The flaps were edged with steel and the boards rimmed with brass. A 'boot' was also attached into which the carbine barrel fitted, and a strap, the 'dragonne', hung from the pommel which passed around the small of the butt. In place of the right-hand holster, brigadiers were sometimes equipped with a holder for a hatchet.

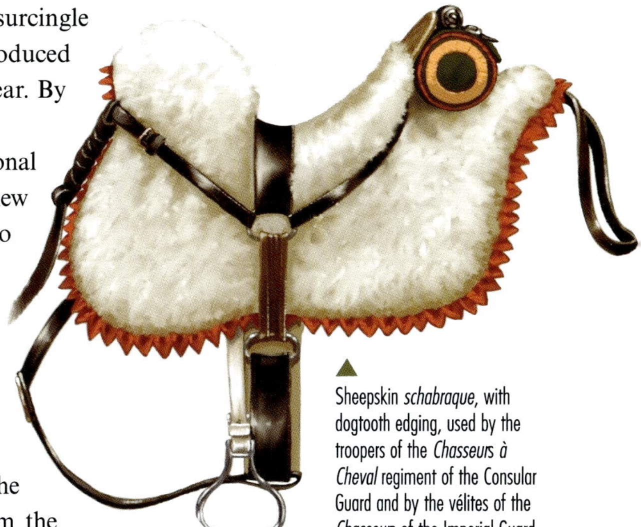

Sheepskin *schabraque*, with dogtooth edging, used by the troopers of the *Chasseurs à Cheval* regiment of the Consular Guard and by the vélites of the *Chasseurs* of the Imperial Guard.

The cloth *schabraque* was dark green edged with gold-yellow lacing that was further piped on the outer edge with scarlet. In the rear corners were *aurore* hunting horns and, at the rear tips, an *aurore* tassel. The tassels were not fitted after 1804, as they made it difficult to fold up the points of the *schabraque*, which was the practice on the march. Otherwise this style of *schabraque* remained in service until 1815, although the horns were replaced by *aurore* crowned eagles in 1806. The *schabraque* was lined with linen and the sides were reinforced with black leather panels where the knees of the rider pressed. In addition to the black leather surcingle, a fawn surcingle was introduced, around 1803, for use on parade with the skin breeches.

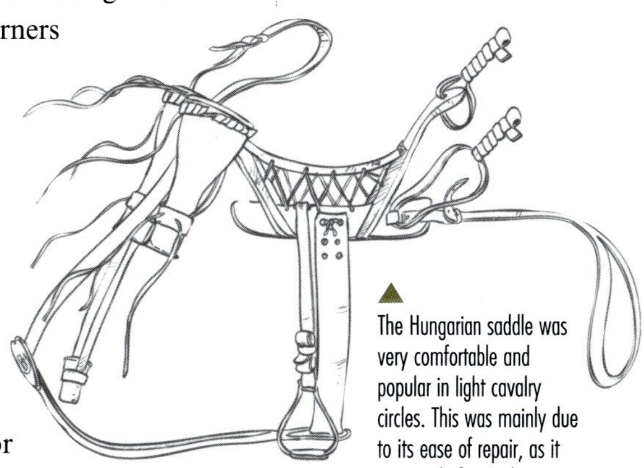

The Hungarian saddle was very comfortable and popular in light cavalry circles. This was mainly due to its ease of repair, as it was made from a large piece of leather, tightened and nailed to a wooden saddletree.

The Hungarian style bridle was black leather, with brass buckles and decorations. These consisted of a curb-chain over the horse's head, a heart-shaped chest ornament, a disc on the forehead, where the

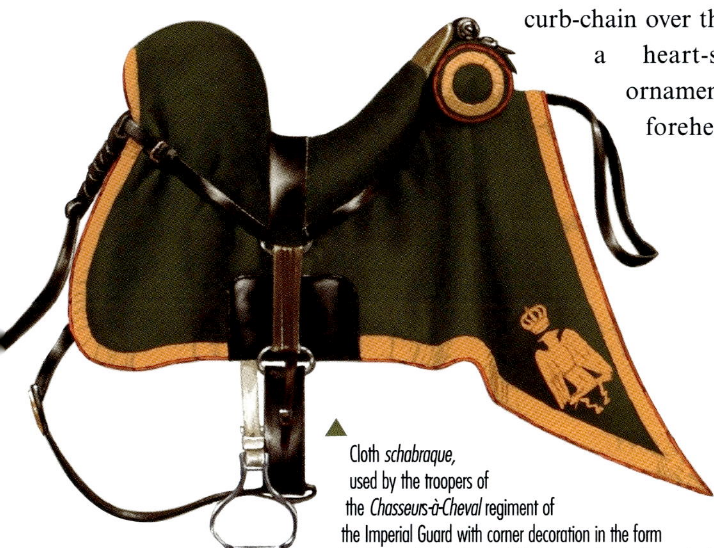

Cloth *schabraque*, used by the troopers of the *Chasseurs-à-Cheval* regiment of the Imperial Guard with corner decoration in the form of the Imperial eagle that, in 1806, replaced the light cavalry hunting horn.

The English saddle, made from a single piece of leather. It was more difficult to repair by one person and required the assistance of a professional saddler.

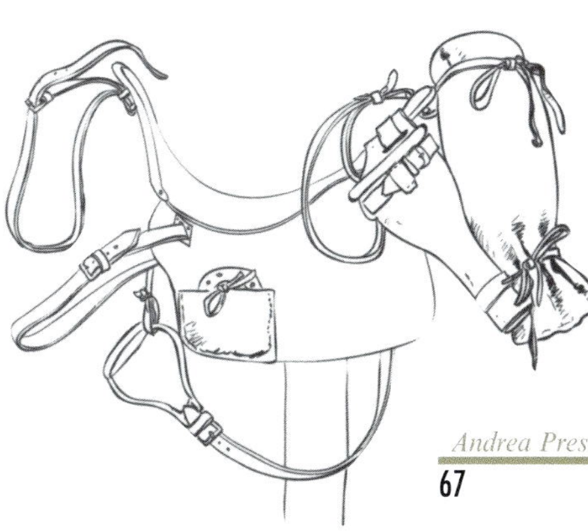

Bit of the *Chasseurs* of the Guard. It was the same model used by the light cavalry. The only difference was the bugle horn ornament, a Chasseurs emblem.

Officer of the *Chasseurs* of the Guard in full dress. A bridle like the one showed on this engraving Martinet is kept in the Musée de la Armée in Paris.

straps crossed, and a neck crescent. The bit was steel with brass bosses stamped with a hunting horn. The hunting horn also appeared on the heart-shaped chest ornament. Attached to the bit was the snaffle rein, usually of black leather for normal use or *aurore* wool for parades. The halter was lined with green cloth, which extended in the form of dogs-teeth at the edges.

The valise was made of green cloth, cylindrical in form, with the ends laced with *aurore* wool and piped scarlet.

STANDARDS

The oath of the army after distribution of the eagles in the Champ de Mars. In the first picture, on the right , an officer of the *Chasseurs* of the Guard in full dress uniform salutes the Emperor and his retinue. (Oil painting by Jacques Louis David).

The standards of the *Chasseurs* can be classified into three types: those carried between 1800 and 1804, between 1804 and 1812 and between 1812 and 1815, excluding the period of the first restoration. During the Consular period, the standard carried by the *Chasseurs* was of crimson damask silk, ornamented with olive leaves and rows of silver-plated "pearls". In the central panel, was a silver-plated hunting horn decorated with gold oak leaves. In the centre of the hunting horn were the letters R.F. (*République Française*) in gold. Under the hunting horn, in golden letters, was the inscription "*Garde des Consuls*". In each corner a small, silver-plated hunting horn was shown. The staff ended in a spear-point, open in the centre and finished off with a gold hunting horn. Tied at the top of the staff, under the spear-point, was a white silk cravat. Next to the cravat was tied a gold cord with gold tassels.

On 5th December 1804 a new standard was introduced into service. This one had a white rhombus in the centre and alternating corners in red and blue. In each corner there was a gold laurel wreath tied with white bows that surrounded a gold hunting horn. The white diamond was adorned with gold leaves and berries and, in it, the following inscription appeared: "L'EMPEREUR DES FRANÇAIS AU REG DE CHASSEURS A CHEVAL DE LA GARDE IMPÉRIALE. On the other face of the standard was either a crowned eagle or the imperial coat of arms. To the left of this, the words "VALEUR ET" and, to

Guidon of the consular period.

Lieutenant *porte-aigle* 1804-1812. The lieutenant has an Eagle escort of a *brigadier* and three Chasseurs. (Watercolor by L. Rousselot, Anne S. K. Brown Collection).

the right, "DISCIPLINE" appeared. Underneath, went the identity of the squadron - for example "1er ESCADRON". The staff for the standard was crowned with a bronze Eagle, the emblem given by the Emperor to his regiments, and whose loss occasioned the greatest dishonour. Following the victory at Austerlitz, the dignitaries of Paris proposed that one of the Guard regiments that had participated in the campaign, should receive gold laurel wreaths to place around the neck of its Eagle. Napoleon agreed, and on 25th November 1807 presented the laurel wreaths. The Eagle stood on a pedestal that, at the front, showed a hunting horn instead of the regimental number, which was the norm in other units.

In July 1813, the standards and Eagles of the 2nd 3rd and 4th squadrons were withdrawn, and a new standard, known as the 1812 model, was introduced to accompany the Eagle of the 1st squadron, thus becoming the standard of the whole regiment. It was square and made up of three vertical bands of the following colors: blue (next to the staff), white and crimson. It was decorated with different elements embroidered in gold on both sides that can be seen more clearly in the accompanying drawing. On one side was the inscription "GARDE IMPÉRIALE L'EMPEREUR NAPOLÉON AU RÉGIMENT DES CHASSEURS À CHEVAL" and, on the other, the military honours of the regiment: "MARENGO, ULM, AUSTERLITZ, JENA, EYLAU, FRIEDLAND, ECKMUHL, ESSLING, WAGRAM, SMOLENSK. MOSKOWA, VIENNE, BERLIN, MADRID, MOSCOU" At the top of the staff hung a tricolour cravat, with a cord of braided gold terminating in two tassels. In the Guard, the standard bearer was a lieutenant and not a veteran sergeant major, as was the custom in the line regiments.

Lieutenant Dieudonné portrait. He was an officer of the *Chasseurs* of the Guard. (Oil on canvas by Théodore Géricault, Museum of the Louvre, Paris).

Eagle and standard, 1813-1814 (obverse and reverse). (Illustration by M.J. Hilpert. The Author's collection).

BIBLIOGRAPHY

BUCQUOY, E. L. *Les Uniformes du Premier Empire. La Garde Impériale. Troupes à cheval*. Jacques Grancher (1977).

BUKHAR, E./McBRIDE, A. *Napoleon's Guard Cavalry*. Osprey (2002).

DEMPSEY, G. *Napoleon's Army 1807-1814 as depicted in the prints of Aaron Martinet*. Arms and Armour (1997).

DUPONT, M. *Guides de Bonaparte et Chasseurs à cheval de la Garde*. Le Livre Chez Vous (2002).

GUETH. F./ ROBICHON. F. *La Grande Armée par Victor Huen*. Herscher (2004).

GRANDIN, F. *Souvenirs historiques du Capitaine Krettly, ancien trompette-major des Guides d'Italie, d'Egypte et des Chasseurs à cheval de la Garde Impériale*. Berlandier, Editeur, Paris (1839).

HEAD, M. *Chasseurs à cheval de la Garde Impériale*. Almark (1978).

JAEGER, G. "Les Chasseurs à cheval de la Jeune Garde", Tradition Magazine, 171.

JOINEAU, A./MONGIN, J. M: *Officers and soldiers of the French Imperial Guard (2. Cavalry, 1804-1805)*. Histoire & Collections (2003).

LACHOUQUE H./ S. K. BROWN. A. *The Anatomy of Glory. Napoleon and his Guard*. Greenhill Books (1997).

PARQUIN, Charles: *Military Memoirs*. Translated and edited by B. T. Jones (1969).

PÉTARD M. "L'Officer des chasseurs à cheval de la Garde", Tradition Magazine, 42 and 43.

PÉTARD M. "Les sabres des Chasseurs à cheval de la Garde", Tradition Magazine, 42 and 43.

PIGEARD A. "Les Chasseurs à cheval de la Garde des Cónsul", Tradition Magazine, 141.

RIGO, *Le Plumet*, plates 8, 26, 27, 136, 179, 195.

ROUSSELOT, L. *L'Armée Française*. Plates 69, 70, 83, 94.

RYAN, E. *Napoleon's Elite Cavalry. Cavalry of the Imperial Guard 1804-1815*. Greenhill Books (1999).

RYAN, E. *Napoleon's Shield and Guardian. The Unconquerable Daumesnil*. Greenhill Books (2003).

VIAU, J. L. "Chasseur à cheval de la Garde, Revue de détail", Tradition Magazine 92.

YOUNG, P. *Chasseurs of the Guard*. Osprey (2002).